FIRST
INSIGHTS
— into —
BUSINESS

Sue Robbins

Librería moncloa

Meléndez Valdés, 65 - 28015 Madrid
Teléf. 91 544 04 82 - Fax 91 549 11 87
http//www.libreriamoncloa.com
e-mail: info@libreriamoncloa.com

TEACHER'S BOOK

Longman

Pearson Education Limited
Edinburgh Gate
Harlow
Essex CM20 2JE
England
and Associated Companies throughout the World.
www.longman-elt.com

First Published in 2000
Third impression 2001
Set in ITC Stone Serif and ITC Stone Sans

Printed in Spain by Gráficas Estella

ISBN 0582 334403

Designed by Cathy May (Endangered Species)
Illustrated by Kathy Baxendale

Acknowledgements
We are grateful to the University of Cambridge Local Examinations Syndicate for kind permission to reproduce adapted extracts from the Handbook to the BEC exam 1998.

The author and publisher would like to thank Linda Davey and James Schofield for commenting on and developing the manuscript.
We would also like to thank Kevin Manton for his work on the test materials and Charlotte Ruse for editing the manuscript.

Teacher's Book Contents:

Introduction to the Teacher's Book

First Insights into Business Teacher's Book is designed to give you practical support in the classroom. Firstly, it provides you with answer keys to Students' Book and Workbook tasks, along with full tapescripts to the Students' Book listening activities. Secondly, the unit-by-unit notes give you additional subject information and company web-site addresses, as well as tips for how to treat the Students' Book activities. On pages 94 to 96, you will also find photocopiable cloze versions of the Key Vocabulary from each unit. These can be used in conjunction with the recorded version. Finally, the Teacher's Book provides you with four photocopiable tests. You can use these simply as progress checks, or as practice to help students prepare for Business English exams.

Exam Preparation

Each test follows the format and content of the UCLES Business English Certificate (BEC) Level 1 examination. It can be very motivating to prepare students for an internationally recognised qualification and these tests will provide them with useful practice. The Workbook writing tasks in each of the Business Writing units give further help in preparing students for the written part of the BEC exam; and the Writing, Reading, Speaking and Listening tasks in the Students' Book encourage students to develop the skills required for the examination.

The following tasks appear in the UCLES BEC Level 1 examination:

WRITING:

PART 1 Form filling (extract information from two short input texts such as memos, notices, ads).

PART 2 Short guided writing (based on a rubric). Write a message or memo.

PART 3 Longer guided writing (read memos, letters, notices, ads. etc.) and write a letter or memo.

READING:

PART 1 Multiple choice reading and vocabulary (read notices, messages, timetables, adverts, leaflets).

PART 2 Matching activities based on vocabulary (read notices, lists, plans, contents pages).

PART 3 Interpreting visual information (read graphs, charts, tables).

PART 4 Reading texts of 150–200 words (adverts, letters, reports, etc.).

PART 5 Reading longer texts 250–300 words (articles, adverts, leaflets).

PART 6 Multiple choice cloze text, testing grammar.

SPEAKING:

PART 1 Interview – giving personal information, agreeing and disagreeing (4–5 mins).

PART 2 Candidate to candidate interaction based on written stimuli (4–5 mins).

LISTENING:

PART 1 Very short conversations or monologues, multiple choice.

PART 2 Short conversations or monologues, gap filling.

PART 3 Listening and writing short answers from telephone conversations.

PART 3 extended conversation, interview or discussion, multiple choice.

Contents

Introduction to the Students' Book

Rationale:

First Insights into Business is a pre-intermediate Students' Book for adult learners of Business English. It aims to provide approximately 120 hours of teaching material. The graded structural syllabus and the focus on systematic vocabulary and skills acquisition provide students with a firm foundation on which to build their business skills. The course is informative, clearly organised and easy to use. It is appropriate for anyone who needs to strengthen their English for use in a business context.

Users of English in a business context need to *know* the rules and systems that underpin the English language. They also need to *use* the language in practice. Without a knowledge of the rules, it is impossible to use the language accurately, and without practising the language in use, it is impossible to learn to express oneself fluently. *First Insights into Business* encourages students to think about the rules that govern grammar, lexis and sentence structure, and offers plentiful opportunities to use the language in a realistic way.

First Insights into Business introduces and explores topics relevant to all students of Business. Each unit looks at a topic such as Customers, Companies, Troubleshooting, Products, the Business Environment, Finance or Competition; each topic is relevant to business people whatever their particular field. Through these broad-ranging topics, a variety of business communication skills are practised; the four language skills, (reading, writing, listening and speaking), are extended; and the students' active vocabulary is developed.

Teaching and learning strategies:

The Students' Book encourages students to be active learners. It adopts an inductive approach to presenting grammar: rather than being asked simply to apply formulas, students are given the presentation material and asked to draw conclusions for themselves. They are then directed to check this with the grammar reference section. In this way students are given, and encouraged to take, a considerable amount of responsibility for their own learning. The teacher's role, therefore, is to support students through the learning process and to encourage them to be curious about language and learning.

The course is designed and structured to offer maximum support to the student. Each unit opens with a focus section, which tells students what they will learn, and closes with a checklist which tests and confirms a student's understanding. Clear rubrics and careful sign-posting help students to work through each unit and in addition, students are regularly referred to the Grammar Reference section which acts to consolidate and reinforce learning.

Methodology:

First Insights into Business is based on a communicative approach to language learning. The core syllabus is structural, and the rules that govern grammar, lexis and sentence structure are presented. Wrapped around the structural syllabus are elements of a functional syllabus, (looking at how different words and structures can perform the same function), and a task-based syllabus, (for example, negotiating, discussing product features or describing trends). Individual work, pair work and group work are all used as classroom techniques and students are asked to bring their own experience and knowledge to bear on the activities.

Use of authentic material:

Students of Business English need to be prepared for texts and situations they will come across in the real world. For this reason, *First Insights into Business* uses authentic reading and listening texts throughout, and teaches students strategies for approaching and decoding material which might not be graded. The texts provide a context for skills development and discussion work, and additionally offer insights into the world of business. The reading texts are taken from the press and business publications and therefore reflect the 'real' world of business, offering a variety of views and opinions. The listening texts offer informed views on a wide range of business-related topics and also provide the stimulus for listening skills development, vocabulary acquisition and discussion work.

The Review units:

Just as the checklist provides an opportunity to reaffirm learning within a unit, the Review units, (which appear after every three Students' Book units), are designed to encourage students to reflect on the learning process. They similarly provide teachers with an opportunity to evaluate what their students have learned, and whether the group, or individuals within it, have gaps in their knowledge or ability. The Review units mainly focus on the grammar, vocabulary and business communication input and should be used in class.

The Key Elements of a Unit:

The following elements appear in each of the 12 Students' Book units. Details of how to exploit an individual section appear in the unit-by-unit notes.

Key Vocabulary

This short passage introduces students to the main theme of the unit and the key items of vocabulary used when discussing it. The key words in **bold** are either followed by a definition, or are defined by their context. Each passage is recorded on cassette so that students can hear how the words are pronounced and how they fit into a pattern of sentence stress. Students can either be asked to study the paragraph before class and to check the meaning of the key words, or the paragraph can be discussed in class as a way into the unit. Alternatively, to find out how much of the vocabulary students already know, the gapped version of the text can be used. (▶ page 94) This gapped version can also be used at the end of the unit as a test to see how much of the vocabulary students can remember.

Lead-in

This section is intended to raise interest in, and awareness of, the main topic of a unit. It helps students bring to mind relevant vocabulary, topic information and personal experience before starting a unit. It also gives the teacher a chance to gauge how confident students are with the topic and how much support they will need with the other activities.

Language Focus and Practice

First Insights into Business follows a grammatical syllabus chosen especially to suit the needs of pre-intermediate to intermediate students, but with a particular bias towards useful business structures. Grammatical items are carefully matched to topics, so for example, Company History focuses on the past simple, Troubleshooting focuses on *should* for recommendations, Travel focuses on the present continuous for fixed arrangements, and so on. Students are often asked to deduce grammar rules from a context. The presentation is followed by a Language Practice section, with a controlled practice task, offering students a high degree of support, followed by a freer activity giving students an opportunity to use the language in a realistic way. All Language Focus sections are supported by and cross-referenced to the Grammar Reference at the back of the Students' Book. Further practice is provided in the Workbook.

Pronunciation

Each Language Focus section is followed by a pronunciation task which makes students aware of how weak forms, contractions, intonation patterns, individual sounds and stress patterns are used in relation to that particular grammatical item.

Writing

The writing syllabus in *First Insights into Business* is carefully designed to focus on the mechanics of writing – an area which is all too often neglected at this level. Students are asked to focus on the structure of sentences and paragraphs, so that, with practice, they learn to put blocks of text together in a more sophisticated way. The writing tasks give students an opportunity to write both accurately and fluently, and additional support is provided through the Grammar Reference section and the Business Writing units (see Workbook). These Business Writing units present a range of business documents in template form and provide an opportunity for students to write in a range of relevant formats.

Reading

Each unit contains an authentic text taken from the press, adverts or from company publications. These texts have been carefully chosen, bearing in mind the clarity of the message, grammatical difficulty, lexical density and syntax. Because they are authentic texts, and have not been especially written for lower intermediate learners, they present language as it is actually used, so may contain vocabulary that students are not familiar with. Where it is necessary for the students' understanding of the text, difficult words have been glossed. On the whole, however, it is the task that has been graded to the students' level rather than the text. It is important, therefore, to encourage students to focus on those parts of the text needed to complete the task, and not to worry about individual words, phrases or structures that are not necessary to their global comprehension of the text. Adopting these strategies will help the students develop 'text-attack' skills which can be transferred to any authentic text.

Listening

Like the Reading sections, the Listening tasks provide students with authentic business texts in the form of unscripted samples of natural English. The interviewers' questions have been specially formulated to elicit straightforward answers, however, and speakers have phrased their answers in a way that avoids complicated grammatical structures. Students need to be encouraged to focus on the task rather than the distractions.

Vocabulary

The vocabulary in a unit is usually taken from the preceding text. The tasks focus on systematic vocabulary development by looking at word-building, synonyms, word partners, compound nouns and compound adjectives. They also extend business vocabulary by looking at word groups related to the topic of the unit. There is a constant recycling of vocabulary and further practice is offered in the Workbook.

Cross-cultural Comparison

This section is designed to raise awareness of how views about business differ around the world. It gives students in multi-lingual groups an opportunity to share their differing viewpoints, and gives students in mono-lingual groups an opportunity to stop and think about how people from other parts of the world may view particular aspects of business. The discussion points are designed to promote an exchange of views and give time for fluency practice and vocabulary revision.

Business Communication

The majority of these sections are oral activities that require students to 'do business' in English. Students are asked to carry out practical tasks such as presenting information, telephoning, describing trends and negotiating. The tasks are carefully structured so that they are appropriate to the students' level, but offer scope to use all the language available to them in a challenging way.

Final Task

The final activity in each unit is designed to allow students to use the business knowledge, grammar and vocabulary that they have acquired during the course of the unit in a realistic way. Usually a speaking task, students work in pairs and give short presentations, conduct telephone conversations, participate in social situations, discuss companies or products and negotiate. The task pulls together the various elements of each unit and consolidates the students' learning.

Introduction to the Workbook

Rationale:

First Insights into Business Students' Book is designed to support a student through the learning process. The Workbook provides further support and contains additional practice material. It offers students a range of self-correcting tasks focusing on language presented in the Students' Book. These tasks recycle both the vocabulary presented in the unit and the topic knowledge the students have gained. They also give further practice of the grammar presented in the unit. The tasks can be done by the student working out of class or as an extension activity during lessons. Students can check their answers in the key provided. You may choose to direct students to a particular practice task if you think they have not fully understood or are not using a structure properly. Alternatively, the students may choose to do a task as a self-directed learning strategy for similar reasons.

Business Writing Units:

A particular feature of the Workbook is its four Business Writing units. They offer guidance and practice in writing business documents. This builds on the structural writing syllabus of the Students' Book, and familiarises students with a wide range of commercial correspondence. The documents are cross-referenced to the 12 Students' Book units and offer realistic practice which is linked to the situations and topic of a unit.

The Business Writing units include practice of:
- form-filling
- writing e-mails
- writing faxes
- writing letters
- writing memos
- writing messages
- writing notices
- writing reports

The Business Writing Reference section at the back of the Workbook provides students with examples of each of these document types. Each example is accompanied by notes on function and information on how to go about writing each document.

Unit 1 Customers

Vocabulary

1   2 e   3 a   4 f   5 g   6 b   7 d

2   1 d – slow   3 b – badly-dressed
       2 c – unfriendly   4 a – unhelpful

3   1 Service   2 service

Language Practice

1   1 e   2 b   3 c   4 d   5 a

2   1 indirect   3 direct   5 direct
       2 direct   4 indirect

3   1 How much is a glass of wine?
       2 Can/Could you tell me when the check-out time is?
       3 Where is the restaurant?
       4 Could you tell me what the rate of exchange for American dollars is?
       5 Do you have a safe for my valuables?
       6 Can/Could you tell me if the restaurant provides children's meals?
       7 Is there a train station near here?
       8 Can/Could you tell me if this is the way to the gym?

Writing

1 Good morning, I'm Dr Hoffman, I'm the hotel doctor, how can I help?
2 Can you tell me how to get to Buckingham Palace?
3 Can I have two beers and a Coca-Cola please?
4 Excuse me, do you speak Polish?
5 Is Christmas Day a Saturday this year?
6 Hello, is that the Hotel Europestar? Can I make a reservation for next March?
7 I want to hire a car. Do you have a BMW?
8 When is the next train to Brussels?
9 There is a special day trip on the River Seine tomorrow. Would you like to come?
10 Can you tell me if the restaurant serves Italian or French food on Wednesday?

Business Communication

1 Would
2 Shall
3 Can
4 Would
5 Can
6 Shall, would

Unit 2 Companies

Vocabulary

1   1 True   3 False
       2 True   4 False

2   1 manufacture   3 launch   5 operation
       2 preparation   4 expand   6 compete

3   1 manufacturer   3 expansion   5 preparations
       2 operates   4 compete   6 launch

Language Practice

1   1 manufactures   4 owns
       2 launches   5 is looking
       3 is expanding

2   Maria and Isabella are marketing officers for Sony. They design advertising campaigns. Today they are not designing campaigns. They are meeting executives from Japan and discussing company strategy.

3   1 Where is the new sales office and shop?
       2 What are they doing at the moment?
       3 Is the new computerised ordering system working?
       4 What does Phil Murphy need?
       5 When does Phil Murphy want someone to come to the sales office in Manchester?

Writing

1 . . . Mercedes Benz is an example of one which manufactures high-quality cars.
2 . . . Others do not.
3 . . . The company also makes shirts and jackets.
4 . . . It has restaurants all over the world.
5 . . . Benetton is one of them.
6 . . . They are found in all major capital cities.

Reading

1   1 f   2 a   3 d   4 e   5 c   6 b

2   1 False   3 True   5 False
       2 False   4 True

Unit 3 Travel
Vocabulary
1
1 is visiting   4 is holding
2 is planning   5 is running
3 booking   6 are throwing

2
1 Swiss   5 Thai
2 France   6 China
3 Greek   7 German
4 Holland   8 Saudi Arabia

3
1 Chinese, Saudi
2 France, Holland
3 Greek, Dutch and German
4 Thailand and China
5 French
6 Swiss

Language Practice
1
1 are visiting   9 is not working
2 are arriving   10 is having
3 are giving   11 is meeting
4 is travelling   12 are attending
5 is visiting   13 are not leaving
6 is not accompanying 14 is returning
7 is staying   15 is not leaving
8 is interviewing

2
1 When is he arriving in Barcelona?
2 He is discussing the new hotel building project with the local management.
3 When is he visiting the building site?
4 He is discussing the plan with local politicians.
5 When is he leaving?

Business Communication
1
1 How do you do?/Pleased to meet you.
2 My name's/I'm Philip.
3 Pleased to meet you.

2 1 b 2 a 3 e 4 c 5 d

3 1 a 2 a

Unit 4 Troubleshooting
Vocabulary
1 g   5 a
2 c   6 e
3 f   7 d
4 b   8 h

Reading
1 True   4 True
2 False   5 False
3 False

Language Practice
1
1 EBP **should use** a troubleshooter.
2 EBP ought **to change** its plans.
3 **Should** Mark Green change the company?
4 EBP ought **to be** a strong company.

2
1 EBP ought to have a new strategy.
2 The company should not lose money.
3 Should they appoint management consultants?
4 Should he use the Progress Consulting Group?

3 2 e 3 c 4 a 5 b 6 d

4
2 EBP should not give only 10% discount. They should give 20%.
3 EBP should not publish 200 different books, it costs them a lot. They should focus on the best selling 100.
4 EBP should not focus their sales only on businesspeople. They should also sell to business students.
5 EBP should not only use traditional sales techniques. They should set up a website for sales.
6 EBP should not only sell in Britain, France, Germany and Spain. They should expand into Eastern European markets.

Writing
1 They should/ought to read 'Writing for Business – The businessperson's guide to good report writing' in order to learn how to write a report.
2 He should/ought to read 'Using a management consultant to analyse your situation' to find out.
3 She should/ought to read 'Seven easy ways to be successful at work' so that she can be successful.
4 They should/ought to read 'The future is now! – Planning a long-term strategy for your business' in order that they can make plans.

Unit 5 Company History
Vocabulary
1 1 e 2 d 3 a 4 f 5 b 6 c

2 1 d 2 c 3 b 4 a

Language Practice
1
/t/: increased, launched, focused, helped, introduced, backed, watched, worked
/d/: arrived, travelled, prepared, offered, planned, tried
/ɪd/: expanded, completed, provided, reported, visited

2
1 took   6 throw   11 leave
2 make   7 met   12 held
3 bought   8 found   13 speak
4 give   9 sell   14 brought
5 ran   10 sent

3
1	makes	8	gave	15	found
2	sends	9	spoke	16	met
3	sent	10	enjoyed	17	were
4	went	11	go	18	threw
5	bought	12	meet	19	left
6	ran	13	don't make		
7	held	14	was		

4
1 When did Karl Toosbuy set up Ecco?
2 What did Ecco do in 1978?
3 Where was Ecco's first overseas factory?
4 When did Vagn Therkel become Managing Director?
5 Why did Ecco begin production in Thailand?

Writing

1
1 Firstly 3 Then 5 Today
2 Secondly 4 Finally

2
1 First of all Eugene Schueller established L'Oréal in 1907. He sold hair dye to hairdressers.
2 Then in 1957 Eugene Schueller died. The new boss Françoise Dalle expanded into manufacturing.
3 After that in 1963 she launched the company on the stock market.
4 Next in 1973 L'Oréal bought the chemicals company Synthélabo.
5 Finally in 1988 the new boss Lindsay Owen-Jones planned to double the size of the company.
6 Today L'Oréal is expanding.

Reading

The correct order is: c, e, a, e, f, b

Unit 6 Retailing
Vocabulary

1 1 a 2 c 3 g 4 d 5 b 6 f 7 e

2
1 manufacturer's
2 supermarket
3 consumers
4 mail-order catalogue
5 department store
6 Shopping Channel
7 Internet

Language Practice One

1 countable: barcode, manufacturer, counter, margin, retail outlet, warehouse, department
uncountable: competition, information, work, luggage, transport, mineral water, packaging

2
1	a	5	a	9	the
2	Ø	6	the, the	10	a
3	the	7	a, the		
4	the, the	8	Ø		

3
a	the, the	e	the, the	i	a
b	the	f	the	j	the
c	the	g	the		
d	a	h	the		

2 a 3 h 4 e 5 b 6 i 7 c 8 f 9 d 10 j

Language Practice Two

1
1 where 4 where 7 which
2 which, where 5 which 8 who
3 who 6 where

2
1 On the second floor there is an electrical appliance department which sells fridges, washing machines and TVs.
2 In the children's play area there are special members of staff who look after the children.
3 Brin Bros is a big department store which has about 10,000 customers every day.
4 On the ground floor there is a cosmetics department where customers can buy all the leading brands such as L'Oréal.

3
1 L'Oréal, which
2 Virgin Atlantic, who
3 DHL, which
4 Sony, which
5 McDonald's, which
6 Bic, which
7 The *Financial Times*, who
8 Benetton, who
9 Levi Strauss, where
10 Ford, which
11 Mercedes Benz, which

Business Communication

1 The correct order is: b, d, a, e, c
2 The correct order is: b, e, c, f, a, d

Unit 7 Products
Vocabulary

1
1 manufacturer 7 worker
2 operator 8 troubleshooter
3 planner 9 reporter
4 programmer 10 wholesaler
5 visitor 11 advertiser
6 analyst

2 **Fast moving consumer goods:**
mineral water, sweets, tissues, cigarettes

Consumer durables:
stereo, microwave oven, telephone, fax machine

3

Features: It is the lightest off-road bike available in this country; easier to stop – with its faster brakes; stronger – with its new design; more comfortable – with its new seat; more stylish – choose from 25 colours

benefits: It gives you all the high quality you expect from a ZEPHYR bike; cheaper than you think

Language Practice One

1 large, round, glass, IKEA dining table
2 Correct.
3 pocket-sized, black, Japanese, steel CD player
4 beautiful, high, dark, French, wooden bookcase
5 stylish, 65 cm, blue Off-Road Roughneck ZC7 bike
6 small, very bright green and yellow, woollen, Benetton jumper
7 upright, yellow, Dyson vacuum cleaner

Language Practice Two

1
1 I think you should buy one at Benetton. They are more stylish and warmer.
2 I think you should get Levis. They are more fashionable and sexier.
3 I think we should buy a Dyson. They are more efficient and more effective.
4 I think you should use DHL. They are faster and more reliable.
5 I think she should read the *Financial Times*. It is more accurate and better.
6 I think you should fly Virgin Atlantic. They are quicker and more comfortable.
7 I think you should get Zephyr Cycles Roughneck ZC7. They are stronger, more comfortable, more stylish and cheaper.

2
1 Peter is buying a Zurich Financial Services Pension. It isn't as convenient as some other pensions, but he thinks it is better.
2 Norbert is buying a Sony Stereo. It isn't as loud as some other stereos, but he thinks it is more stylish.
3 Anna is buying a Skoda car. It isn't as luxurious as some other cars, but she thinks it is more reliable.
4 Nicholas is buying a Dyson vacuum cleaner. It isn't as light as some other vacuum cleaners, but he thinks it is more efficient.
5 Maria is buying a new EBP business book. It isn't as easy to understand as some other books, but she thinks it is more useful.

Reading

1	True	5	False	9	True
2	True	6	False	10	False
3	False	7	False		
4	False	8	False		

Writing

1
2	h	5	a	8	e
3	d	6	g		
4	f	7	b		

2
2 All serious businesspeople read the *Financial Times* **because** it provides accurate and reliable information about business./All serious businesspeople read it **because** the *Financial Times* provides accurate and reliable information about business.
3 The company's strategy was very unclear. **As a result** the new Managing Director called in a firm of troubleshooters.
4 The new parent company wanted to boost sales **so** they opened a website.
5 The company wanted to cut production costs. They **therefore** invested in new technology for the factory which was cheaper.
6 The Roughneck ZC7 is cheaper and lighter than other bikes **so** it is the most popular with customers.
7 **Because** e-commerce is becoming more popular, shops are losing business./Shops are losing business **because** e-commerce is becoming more popular.
8 There can be a big culture gap between people from different countries. **As a result** it can be hard to do business abroad.

Unit 8 People
Vocabulary

1
salary:	tick Bruno
achievement:	tick Michael
social interaction:	tick Charles
status:	tick Patricia

2
1 higher productivity   3 job satisfaction
2 style of management   4 asset

Language Practice One

1
1 He is going to like the new manager.
2 She is not going to like her new job.
3 Are they going to Tokyo next month?

2
1 She is going to leave next week because of the confrontational culture in her present job.
2 They are going to stay because of the job satisfaction here.
3 I am not going to leave because of the social interaction at my office.
4 She is not going to be happy because of the competition at work.
5 They are going to be satisfied because of the flatter organisation with their present employer.

Reading

1   1 b   2 c   3 d   4 a

2   1 False   2 False   3 True   4 False

Language Practice Two

1
1 will happen   5 will not be
2 will not like   6 will become
3 will help   7 will use
4 will mean   8 will not be able to

a True   c False   e True
b False   d False   f True

2
1 **He will not go** to Hungary next month.
2 Correct
3 **Will she meet** the local workers when she comes here?
4 Correct
5 Correct
6 **It will not be** possible for us all to go on the trip.

Writing

1   Beatrice will like the location and the teamwork at Euro Bank. However she won't like the salary and the business travel.
2   Although Carmen will like the individual responsibility and the location at London Bank, she won't like the weekend working and the exams.
3   Denis will like the training and the exams at London Bank but he won't like the location.
4   Jordi won't like the individual responsibility at NY Corp. However he will like the salary and job security.
5   Although Henri will like the location and job security at NY Corp, he won't like the individual responsibility.
6   Stefania will like living and travelling in Europe but she won't like the lack of responsibility and low salary at Euro Bank.
7   Although Juliet will like the training and the chance to get more qualifications she won't like the individual responsibility and lack of travelling at London Bank.
8   Daniel will like the responsibility and weekend work at NY Corp. However he won't like living outside Europe and the lack of travel.

Unit 9   Business Environment

Vocabulary

1
analysis   analytical unanalytical
employment   employer   employed   unemployed
unemployment employee   employable unemployable

2
1 economic   4 employees
2 uneconomic   5 unemployable
3 unemployment   6 analytical

3
1 d   4 e   7 h
2 c   5 a   8 b
3 f   6 g

Reading

1   In Liverpool and Lyons.
2   Eastern Europe.
3   Because of the state of the Western European economy.
4   No, they are not.
5   No, they don't.

Language Practice One

1 probably   4 probably   7 Perhaps
2 Perhaps   5 may   8 might be
3 might be   6 probably   9 may

Language Practice Two

1
1 makes   6 are sold
2 are made   7 is imported
3 are produced 8 is
4 are employed 9 needs
5 are supported 10 are manufactured

2
1 Clothes are made in Europe.
2 Good clothes are made by other companies in Asia.
3 Many changes to the business environment are caused by new technology.
4 Before clothes leave the factory they are checked carefully at quality control.
5 Lots of orders are taken through the company's new website.

Writing

1   In Eastern Europe the company will pay low taxes, and in addition it will gain from good availability of labour.
2   In Western Europe the company pays high taxes, it experiences poor availability of labour too.
3   In Eastern Europe the company will gain from good availability of labour. It will also benefit from easy access to raw materials.
4   In Western Europe the company pays high labour costs, it suffers poor access to raw materials as well.
5   In Eastern Europe the company will achieve low labour costs, and in addition it will gain easy access to raw materials.
6   In Western Europe the company experiences a weak economy. It also suffers poor access to raw materials.
7   In Eastern Europe the company will benefit from a strong economy, it will find good availability of labour as well.
8   In Western Europe the company experiences a weak economy, it suffers poor availability of labour too.

Business Communication

1　b　　　2　c

Unit 10　Finance
Vocabulary

Across:　3 rate　5 annual　7 offshore　8 results
Down:　1 fall　2 turnover　4 tax year　5 account
　　　　　6 profit

Language Practice One

1　1 a　2 b　3 b　4 a　5 c　6 a　7 c

2　1 a　2 b　3 a

3　2 third　3 fifth

Language Practice Two

1　arose　　　3　raise
2　rose　　　4　rise

Writing

1　Rephrasing:　a, b, c, f
　　Exemplifying:　d, e, g

2　2 f　3 c　4 g　5 d　6 a　7 e

Business Communication

1　1 a　2 d　3 j　4 e　5 i　6 b　7 f　8 c
　　9 h　10 g

2　1 'm certain/sure that　　4 'm certain/sure that
　　2 'm certain/sure that　　5 'm certain/sure
　　3 might/may　　　　　　6 it's likely that

Unit 11　Corporate Responsibility
Vocabulary

1　1 c　2 b　3 d　4 e　5 a

2　1 ethical
　　2 environmental
　　3 a powerful
　　　b powerless
　　4 sceptical

3　1 ethical　　　　　　　　3 powerless, powerful
　　2 environment, environmental　4 sceptical

Language Practice One

1　1 is, will adopt
　　2 adopts, will pay
　　3 are, will support
　　4 support, will not be
　　5 are not, will fall
　　6 fall, will need

2　2 What will happen if UCG adopt an ethical policy?
　　3 What will people do if they are concerned about the environment?
　　4 What will happen if consumers support the campaign?
　　5 What will happen if the Nimrod and Achilles brands are not successful?
　　6 What will happen if UCG's profits fall?

Language Practice Two

1

verb + *-ing*:	like, dislike, delay, finish, include, practise, risk, suggest
verb + *to* infinitive:	arrange, decide, expect, help, manage, promise, plan, want
verb + infinitive without *to*:	could, might, must, should

2　1 to proceed　　9 to meet
　　2 to delay　　　10 realise
　　3 listen　　　　11 to introduce
　　4 being　　　　12 paying
　　5 to avoid　　　13 losing
　　6 arguing　　　14 to change
　　7 to negotiate　　15 to return
　　8 arrange　　　16 charging

Reading

1 False　　　3 True　　　5 False
2 False　　　4 False

Writing

1　Both AFG and Zephyr Cycles have good working conditions in Europe.
2　Both UCG and International Fibres use child labour.
3　Both Euro Bank and International Fibres have a poor environmental record.
4　Both Zephyr Cycles and International Fibres pay on time.
5　Neither AFG nor Zephyr Cycles use child labour.
6　Neither London Bank nor UCG have good working conditions in Europe.
7　Neither Euro Bank nor International Fibres have a good environmental record.
8　Neither London Bank nor UCG pay on time.

Unit 12 Competition

Vocabulary

1
1	c	4	g
2	f	5	e
3	a	7	d

2 1 market leader 3 enter new markets
2 market share 4 upmarket

Language Practice One

1 1b Q Has he given a presentation at Yves Saint Laurent?
A No, he hasn't.
2 Q Has he visited Mme Orleans at the Industry Ministry?
A No, he hasn't.
3 Q Has he found an office in Paris?
A Yes, he has.
4 Q Has he interviewed the French distribution companies?
A No, he hasn't.
5a Q Has he signed contracts with the French lawyers?
A Yes, he has.
5b Q Has he signed contracts with the French accountants?
A No, he hasn't.

2 1 Eco Save has closed a chemical factory.
2 AFG has completed a move to Poland.
3 Zephyr Cycles has won an Eco Prize.
4 Euro Bank has recruited the best business students again.
5 The *Financial Times* has voted Georgio Pujol businessman of the year.
6 Computers have made 250 staff redundant at London Bank.
7 Asian firms have penetrated Euro markets
8 Skoda has launched an upmarket model..

3 3 Q Has Georgio Pujol ever been to Germany?
A No, he's never been there.
4 Q Has Georgio Pujol ever been to Spain?
A Yes, he has. He's been there twice.
5 Q Has Georgio Pujol ever been to Greece?
A Yes, he has. He's been there once.
6 Q Has Georgio Pujol ever been to Turkey?
A No, he's never been there.

Language Practice Two

1 For: a long time, years, ages, ten weeks, two months, five minutes, three hours, more than six years, too long

Since: Christmas, the holidays, 1960, last March, half past three, the 1970s, England won the World Cup, the office closed, I came here

2 1 F&D Chemicals' market share has increased _____ (steadily).
2 F&D Chemicals' production costs have fallen. _____ (dramatically).
3 The number of employees has remained steady.

3
1	joined	9	has reduced
2	has been	10	closed
3	has been	11	invested
4	began	12	has increased
5	joined	13	began
6	have risen	14	has forced
7	has happened	15	has been
8	has been		

Business Communication

1 c 2 e 3 a 4 d 5 h 6 f 7 g 8 b

The correct order is: 7, 2, 6, 1, 5, 3, 8, 4

Customers

Further information about some of the companies mentioned in this unit is available at these websites:

Kwik Fit	http://www.kwik-fit.com
Marks and Spencer	http://www.marks-and-spencer.com
British Airways	http://www.british-airways.com

If your students have access to the Internet, you could ask them to do research from the various company websites.

Key Vocabulary

🔲 **1.1** Read this section through with the students. Make sure that the students can pronounce as well as use the key words by playing the recorded version. It may be useful to ask the students to provide examples to confirm they understand these terms.

You may like to ask students to complete the cloze version of the Key Vocabulary. (► page 94) You could give it to your students to see how many of the words and phrases they know before beginning the unit, or alternatively, because cloze tests can be very challenging for students, after they have completed the unit, as a check.

Ask students to think of five situations where they are customers, e.g. college cafeteria, bank, telephone company etc. What do they think of the customer service? Are they loyal customers? If so, why (or why not)?

► **For more practice see Workbook page 4**

Lead-in

Ask if the students have heard of any of these companies. If they have find out what they know.

Cross-cultural comparison

1

Suggest sudents do this according to acceptable standards in their own country and in multi-national classes, compare their answers with someone from a different country.

2

🔲 **1.2**

TAPESCRIPT 1.2:

Stephen Nicholl:
One thing that does irritate me is when I ask somebody for some information about a product or a service and they don't know the answer, but they don't say 'I'm sorry I don't know the answer to this, I'll find someone who does know the answer.' – they try to answer it themselves and it's really a waste of time for everybody concerned.

KEY:
The man describes situation 3.

Language Focus

1 🔲 **1.3** Explain to students that they are going to listen to someone phoning a health and fitness club. Give them time to compare their ideas with a partner. Discuss the answers as a class.

TAPESCRIPT 1.3:

(**R**= Receptionist, **TS** = Tim Saunders)

R: Good afternoon, Hi-tone Health and Fitness Centre. How may I help you?

TS: Oh, hello. I'm thinking of joining a fitness centre. Could you give me some information about Hi-tone?

R: Yes, of course.

TS: So first of all, could you tell me how much it costs?

R: Is it just for you?

TS: Yes.

R: OK. It's £550 for a year and for that you can use all the facilities. We have a fully-equipped gym, saunas, steambaths and a swimming pool and squash courts. And you can pay in monthly instalments if you like.

TS: Right. And what are your opening hours?

R: We're open 7 days a week from 6.30 in the morning to 10 every evening.

TS: OK. And how does it work? I mean, could you tell me what the procedure is.

R: You have a fitness assessment with an instructor, then we design a fitness programme for you... and we review your programme every two months.

TS: That's good. Could you tell me what qualifications your instructors have?

R: Oh, they are all fully qualified and very experienced.

TS: Uh-huh. Do you have fitness classes as well?

R: Yes, we do. We run six different types of fitness class. There's one every evening except Saturdays.

TS: Right, and what about the class size? Is there a maximum number in each class?

R: Yes, the maximum number of people in a class is fifteen. But there are usually only about eight people in a class.

TS: And can I come and see if I like it? Do you offer a free introductory session?

R: Yes, we do. I can book you in for that, if you like.

TS: Yes, thank you. Just one final question. Can you tell me if it's possible to bring guests?

R: Yes, when you're a member you can bring one guest. It costs £7.50 a visit.
TS: OK. Can I book an introductory session for next week?
R: Sure. Could you give me your name and a telephone number?

2 Check that students understand the difference between direct and indirect questions. Play recording 1.3 again for students to tick the questions asked. Check answers as a class.

KEY:

1 b	2 a	3 b	4 b
5 a	6 a	7 a	8 b

You may like to refer the students to Grammar Reference page 155 at this point.

3 It would be a good idea to go through the questions as a class as this is the first Language Focus. In this way, students will learn how to approach the Language Focus questions in later units; they can work through them on their own and then compare either with a partner or as a class. If students do the exercise on their own, you should first check that they understand the term *auxiliary verb*.

KEY:

All the statements are true.

Pronunciation

1 🔲 1.4 Play each question and answer to isolate the strong and weak sounds and drill if required. Students should then practise the questions and answers in pairs.

2 KEY:
The weak form is the normal unstressed form. We use the strong form for short answers.

Language Practice

1 and **2**
Pre-teach *objectives*. Students could do this activity on their own then ask a partner the questions to see if they agree.

3 🔲 1.5 Play the tape to check answers.

TAPESCRIPT 1.5:

I: Do you do any exercise at the moment?
TS: No, I don't. And the problem is I sit at my desk all day.
I: What are your favourite sports?
TS: I like swimming and I enjoy a game of squash now and again!

I: Could you tell me if you have any medical problems or injuries?
TS: No, I'm very healthy, thank goodness.
I: How often do you want to come to the Centre?
TS: Probably three or four times a week.
I: Can you tell me what your objectives are?
TS: I want to get fit and I want to lose a few kilos too.
I: And what do you do?
TS: I'm a business analyst.

KEY:

1 d iii	3 c vi	5 b ii
2 e v	4 a iv	6 f i

4 Students who are already confident with these question forms can do roleplay straightaway. Alternatively, less confident students could work first in pairs and share their role with a partner.

➤ **For more practice see Workbook page 5**

Writing

Your students may not know some of the items mentioned in the lists. This is not as important as getting the general point.

1 Encourage students to work through the list in pairs to come up with as many rules as possible for when to use capital letters. Check answers as a class.

KEY:

1 Names and titles	7 Festival days
2 Job titles	8 Names of countries,
3 Street and place names	nationalities and languages
4 Names of cities	9 Famous buildings
5 Geographical features	10 Names of companies
6 Days and months	11 Acronyms

2 Ask the students to correct the letter in pairs or small groups. You may like to ask them to write their letter on OHT for whole group analysis.

➤ **See Workbook page 71 for letter writing**

KEY

> Hi-tone
> Health and Fitness Centre
> Rushmoor Hotel, Crawley, West Sussex
> phone/fax: 011293 4000064
>
> 20 July
> Mr T Saunders
> 25 Crawley Road
> Reigate
>
> Dear Mr Saunders
>
> We are delighted to enclose your membership card to Hi-tone Health and Fitness Centre. On your next visit one of our instructors will guide you through your new fitness programme and show you how to use the equipment in the gym. Please phone to arrange a time convenient to you.
> We hope to welcome you to our many social events. We have an action-packed programme over the summer starting with a 1970s disco evening on 4 June.
> As a member of the Centre you are entitled to a 15% discount on food and drink. The sports bar is also equipped with Sky TV. We look forward to seeing you soon.
>
> Julian Darleston
> Assistant Manager

Listening

1 🔲 **1.6a** Before listening, elicit what students can remember about First Direct from the lead-in. Then find out what they know about Marks and Spencer. Ask students to read questions 1–4 and play the recording for them. Encourage students to check their answers in pairs and if necessary play the tape again. Check the answers as a class.

Check students understand all the words in question 2 and that they can pronounce *courteous, co-operative* and *professional* with the correct word stress.

TAPESCRIPT 1.6:

(**AH:** Ann Hislop, **SN:** Stephen Nicholl)

Int: So, Ann and Stephen. I'd like to ask you some questions about customer service. Are there any companies which you are loyal to?

AH: I am fantastically loyal to Marks and Spencers.

SN: I'm also quite loyal to Marks and Spencers. If you buy presents for people and they don't like them, they can take the things back and they can exchange them.

Int: So what's the attitude of the staff like at Marks and Spencers?

AH: Friendly ...

SN: Yeah.

AH: ... helpful,

SN: professional,

AH: co-operative, loyal to their company. They obviously enjoy working there most of the time. Yeah I don't know how they manage it, but they have a very friendly, er, staff.

Int: What about the quality of their of their products?

AH: Fantastic.

Int: Are there any other companies which you're very loyal to?

SN: One company that I am loyal to, I think, is my bank which is First Direct.

Int: And why's that?

SN: Well, first of all they're extremely convenient to use. I do all my banking is over the phone and I can do this at any time of the day. I can find out how much money there is in my account, I can pay all my bills. I don't, I don't send any bills through the mail, erm and also they're very very professional, they're very friendly.

KEY:

1	c	**3**	Fantastic
2	a c e g h	**4**	b

2 🔲 **1.6b** Before students complete exercise 2, ask them to read the summary and see if they can fill in any of the gaps before they listen again.

KEY:

¹loyal ²convenient (to use) ³phone ⁴account ⁵bills ⁶professional ⁷friendly

► **For further vocabulary practice see Workbook page 4**

3 KEY:

a	unfriendly	**e**	unprofessional
b	discourteous	**f**	badly-dressed
c	unhelpful	**g**	unco-operative
d	slow	**h**	disloyal (to the company)

KEY

```
d i s c o u r t e o u s . t h m u
i y a c m n r p l u n k c b v n
s l o w i f b e i m p o l a t c
l a k a d n i f a t r w b a i o
o g e p n i e z o d o l t r a o
y s o i o e s o e c f e n r y p
a c d e i n s o b g e s o d l e
t d e i d q w q v s s p n i r
b e m o l y m x z o r i v r e a
o y i t u c k b r o x o b r k t
a n o a h r n m i t n v t k a i
s d c s u w p n w c a u e s a v
m g u n h e l p f u l e h o e
b a d l y d r e s s e d h l n w
```

Reading

COMPANY NOTE The name Kwik-Fit is from *Quick fit.*

Before students do the reading exercise check they understand *guarantee.* Direct their attention to the illustration to show them what *exhaust, puncture* and *valve* mean.

1 Encourage students not to read every word but to find the information to complete the gaps.

2 Students need to read the text more carefully here to match the benefits to the paragraphs.

KEY:

1	Open 7 days per week	**a**	long hours
2	Independence	**c**	customer choice
3	Free puncture repair service	**d**	free service
4	Express tyre-fitting	**b**	fast service
5	Extended guarantees	**e**	peace of mind

Vocabulary

Follow the activity as directed in the Students' Book.

1 KEY:

1 d   2 c   3 b   4 a

2 KEY:

1 late-night openings   3 customer helpline
2 lifelong guarantee   4 Kwik-Fit fitter

Business Communication

1 Direct students' attention to the three situations in the illustrations. Ask them what is happening then let them do the exercise individually. Check the phrases are correctly underlined, then write them on the board:

KEY:

1 Would you like ...?
2 Would you like ...?
3 Shall I ...?

2 🔲 1.7 Play the tape and check the students have understood the offers and responses in general terms.

TAPESCRIPT 1.7:

Conversation 1
Secretary: Good morning. RTA, Lisa speaking, how may I help you?
Customer: Oh, hello. Erm, I have an appointment to see David Barnes on Tuesday, but I'm afraid I can't make it then. Would it be possible to change it?
Secretary: Just one moment. Err, yes, I can give you an earlier appointment, if you like.
Customer: Yes, that would be very helpful. Thank you.

Conversation 2
Secretary: Mr Smith will be with you in a minute. Would you like to take a seat?
Customer: Thank you.
Secretary: Would you like a coffee?
Customer: Thank you very much. That would be very nice. Black, no sugar please.

Conversation 3
Secretary: Shall I call a taxi for you?
Customer: That's very kind of you, but I think I'll get some exercise and walk.

KEY:

1 to give him an earlier appointment
  to get him a coffee
  to call a taxi

2 accepts   accepts   refuses

3 Before students listen to the three conversations again, draw a table on the board with the headings *offer* and *accept/refuse*. Students listen to the conversations and complete the table. Check their answers and write them up on the board. Drill for correct stress and intonation.

KEY:

Offer	Accept / Refuse
I can give you an earlier appointment, if you like.	Yes, that would be very helpful. Thank you.
Would you like a coffee?	Thank you very much.
Shall I call a taxi for you?	That's very kind of you, but ...

4 Students can do this on their own and check their answers with a partner.

KEY:

1 d   3 f   5 e
2 c   4 b   6 a

5 Ask students to prepare exchanges for each of these situations and ask different pairs to demonstrate one of their exchanges to the rest of the class.

Final Task

Suggest all Student As should prepare together and likewise Student Bs. As students prepare and roleplay speaking tasks, walk around the classroom monitoring and giving feedback. You could choose to collect common mistakes anonymously to put on the board at the end of the activity for students to correct. You could also try recording the exchanges so that students can listen critically to themselves.

Checklist

KEY:

1 Customers buy from the same company again and again.
2 Apologising to customers/after-sales support to customers/being helpful/long opening hours
3 Personal apologies and gifts
4 Free banking and £15 when you open an account.
5 Can you tell me if you have a code of practice?

unit 2

Companies

Further information about some of the companies mentioned in this unit is available at these websites:

Virgin: hhtp://www.virgin.com
McDonald's: http://www.mcdonald.com
Pearson: http://www.pearson.com

If your students have access to the Internet, you could ask them to do research themselves from the various company websites.

Key Vocabulary

2.1 Read through this section with the students. Make sure that the students can pronounce as well as use the words by playing the recorded version. It may be useful to ask the students what they think is involved in some of the functions, such as marketing. A simple diagram of a company structure, real or imaginary, may help explain the last three terms.

You may like to use the cloze version of the Key Vocabulary. (▶ page 94)

▶ **For more practice see Workbook page 7**

Lead-in

1 Direct students' attention to the photos. Ask them to identify the companies.

KEY:

1 Reuters   3 DHL
2 McDonald's 4 EMI

2 Before students do the matching exercise, write the names of the companies on the board. Ask students to discuss in pairs what they know about the companies. Students then complete the exercise in pairs and check answers as a class. Check students understand that *produce* is followed by the name of the product; *provide* is used before describing a service. Check also that they can pronounce *provide* and *produce* correctly.

Do they use any products/services from these companies?

KEY:

1 Reuters 3b   3 DHL 4d
2 EMI 1c   4 McDonald's 2a

3 It might help to ask the students if they know the following:
Where and when these companies were established. What their main products/services are.

Students write a brief profile of three of the companies. As a follow up, each group could read out one of the profiles and the others could guess which company they are describing.

If you have Internet access, students could check their answers this way.

Language Focus

1 As a lead-in, if your students are already working, ask them how they found out about the job, e.g. newspaper ad, ad on the Internet, etc. Ask students to read the ad quickly and encourage them to discuss whether they think it is an interesting job.

2 Remind students that it is not necessary to understand all the vocabulary in the ad, but to select the information they need to complete the paragraph. You might want to do a quick check after they have completed the exercise that they understand all the recruitment vocabulary, e.g. *recruit, apply, skills, experience, CV, applicant, candidate, shortlisted*.

KEY:

1 Finance Manager
2 Granada Media Group
3 produces
4 co-finances
5 film finance experience
6 good communication skills
7 the ability to work under pressure
8 the Controller of Finance
9 letter (application in writing)
10 CV

3 Ask students to complete the sentences and then discuss questions 3 and 4 in pairs. Check answers as a class.

KEY:

1 produces ... co-finances   2 are looking for
3 non-permanent or
  current activity = present continuous.
4 a fact or a permanent activity = present simple.

Students could read through the Grammar Reference for homework.

Pronunciation One

2.2, 2.3

KEY:

a = /z/   b = /ɪz/   c = /s/

22

3 KEY:

1 Verbs that end in /p/, /t/, /k/, /f/ we pronounce the final 's' /s/
2 Verbs that end in /s/, /z/, /ʃ/, /tʃ/, /dz/ we pronounce the final 's' /ɪz/
3 Verbs that end in all other sounds we pronounce the final 's' /z/

Once students have completed the rules, suggest that they test each other using the verbs in exercise 2 – one says the infinitive form, and the other gives the third person singular form. Alternatively, you could do it as a quick test.

► **For more practice see Workbook page 8**

Language Practice

1 Students discuss the companies' activities in pairs then discuss as a class. Check that they are using the vocabulary correctly.
e.g. *A pharmaceutical company develops new medicines.*

2 🖭 2.4 You might want to stop after the description of the first company to give students time to write down notes. Discuss in pairs and then listen again.

TAPESCRIPT 2.4:

(**BA** = Business analyst)

BA: Right, so the first company I want to look at is a pharmaceuticals company. It develops and manufactures a wide range of medicines and it's currently developing a new drug against asthma. Well, as you all know, more and more people are suffering from asthma so they hope to make a healthy profit from this drug.

The company is currently preparing to launch a TV advertising campaign. As you may know, it is illegal to show drugs on TV, so the campaign focuses on the illnesses not the drugs. It will be interesting to see public reaction to this.

BA: So let's have a look at the second company. This company is a cable operator. Well, it provides cable television to thousands and thousands of homes, but it wants to expand and it's developing a new high-speed Internet service. Now, this service uses cables not phone wires and this means it is very fast – 100 times faster than a normal phone line. As you know, the number of people who are using the Internet is growing and growing and everyone wants instant information so this is a company with a great future.

NOTE Asthma is a disease that makes breathing difficult.

	PHARMACEUTICAL COMPANY	CABLE OPERATOR
KEY:		
What the company does	It develops and manufactures a wide range of medicines.	It provides cable television to thousands of homes.
Current activities	It's currently preparing to launch a TV advertising campaign.	It's currently developing a new high-speed Internet service.

► **For the vocabulary in question 2 there is a practice activity in the Workbook page 7**

Reading

1 This task is designed to develop scanning skills, so encourage the students to do the first part as quickly as possible. You could give them a time limit of one minute.
Tell students to have a quick look at the ad and answer questions 1 and 2. Find out how they know that it is a recruitment ad, e.g. mentions salary, says how to apply, and check they understand *graduate*.

KEY:

1 a   2 a The intended readers are business graduates.

2 This requires more intensive reading so give students enough time to read carefully.

KEY:

1 The FT Group is part of Pearson plc.
2 Publishing, TV production, broadcasting and electronic/multimedia business.
3 a   newspapers and magazines
   d   financial information,
   f   electronic information,
   g   business information.
4 The *Financial Times*, *Les Echos*, *Recoletos*.
5 They are planning to recruit up to six business graduate trainees.
6 strategic planning, product development, editorial, marketing, advertisement sales
7 Ability to think innovatively and practically, a high degree of business awareness, good communication skills, ambition, a wide range of interests and experience.
8 Personal qualities: ability to think, interests, ambition, Skills/knowledge: business awareness, communication skills and experience
9 15 months
10 Equality of opportunity

Vocabulary

Word building

1 Encourage students to use a monolingual dictionary to check their answers. Copy the table onto the board and elicit students' answers. Mark on word stress and drill if necessary.

Point out that *advertisement* is often shortened. Find out if students know to what (*ad, advert*).

KEY:

1 produce	3 develop	5 advertise
2 provide	4 market	

2 KEY:

1 market	3 develop	5 production
2 product	4 market	6 advertise

Listening

1 Before students listen, discuss what they know about the companies with a partner and fill in any of the information they already know.

2 🔲 2.5 Stop the tape after each section for students to complete their notes. Give students time to compare their answers in pairs and then play the tape again.

NOTE Tell students that Mercedes-Benz is part of Daimler Chrysler before listening.

See page 25 for Key to Listening 1 and 2.

TAPESCRIPT 2.5:

(**TA**: Tom Armstrong, **RH**: Rachel Humphries)

RH: So Tom, what do you know about the Virgin Group?

TA: They're a very large group, erm, they exist in a lot of different sectors and they're run by Richard Branson – they're British.

RH: Yes, yeah and they, erm they produce, er Virgin Cola, don't they?

TA: Yeah and I think they're also famous for the airline, the Virgin Atlantic.

RH: Um, and er they have a radio station – Virgin Radio.

TA: Yeah, and they still have the megastores, and I think they have megastores all over the world now.

RH: Yes.

TA: Selling videos, music.

Stop tape

What do you know about Benetton?

RH: Well, they're Italian, and they're very successful clothing manufacturers.

TA: I think they produce sportswear now.

RH: Yes, that's right – sportswear, and erm, another, they have another trademark called Sisley, which produces more expensive clothing.

Stop tape

TA: And Mercedes-Benz – do you know anything about them?

RH: Well they manufacture expensive, luxury cars erm and they're, erm German I think, or maybe German-American now, perhaps.

TA: I think they're part of the Daimler-Chrysler Group, which again is a large group ... I've heard that they also produce a very small car called The Smart.

RH: Oh right, it's good for the towns and cities.

TA: Yeah.

Stop tape

RH: And what about Sony?

TA: Oh Sony, they're, they're as far as I know they're still the world leaders in electronics, and produce, for example, the Sony Walkman.

RH: Mmm, and they're Japanese.

TA: Yeah.

RH: And er, what else do they produce? ... computer games.

TA: Yeah, and they also do music now; they did the music for the film *Titanic*.

Writing

1 Read through the example as a class. Students complete the exercise on their own or in pairs.

KEY:

1 *one* = companies (noun)
2 *others* = companies (noun)
3 *these* = clients (noun)
4 *The Company* = The EMI Group (noun)
5 *It* = DHL (noun)
6 *They* = HMV stores (noun)
7 *one* of them = fast food companies (noun)

2 KEY:

1 These 2 They 3 They / The group
4 one of them

3 Students can do this on their own or in pairs.

Business Communication

1 🔲 2.6 Direct students to the questions under the pictures. Check they understand what *sectors* and *brand names* mean. Students discuss in pairs what they think the answers are before they listen.

TAPESCRIPT 2.6:

Speaker: A lot of you will have heard of this next multinational's products, but I suspect that fewer of you will have heard of the company itself; LVMH.

First of all, what does LVMH stand for? The answer is the world's leading luxury goods group; Louis Vuitton Moët Hennessy.

KEY TO LISTENING 1 and 2:				
	Virgin	Benetton	Daimler Chrysler	Sony
Nationality	British	Italian	German–American	Japanese
Product(s)	Virgin Cola Virgin Atlantic Virgin Radio Virgin Megastore	clothes sportswear	expensive, luxury cars The Smart car	electronics computer games music
Other information		Trademark – Sisley	Mercedez-Benz is part of the group	Sony Walkman

So what does the group do? Well, of course, it specialises in luxury products.... and it operates in a number of sectors. As you can see from the chart, these are wines and spirits, fashion and leather goods, fragrances and cosmetics and selective retailing. Look at the brand names in each sector. Each sector includes world-famous names.

Let's look first at wines and spirits. LVMH is the world leader in champagne production with brands such as Dom Perignon, Moët & Chandon and Pommery.

KEY:
1 Luis Vuitton Moët Hennessy
2 wines & spirits, fashion and leather goods, fragrances and cosmetics, selective retailing
4 up-market

Pronunciation Two

2 ▭ 2.7 Students listen to the tape and mark the stressed syllables. Ask students to check their answers in pairs and practise saying the sentences to each other. To check answers, write the sentences up on the board and ask students to read the sentence out with the correct stress pattern. Mark the syllables they stress on the board and check that the other students agree. If there are any problems, you may want to play the tape again.

TAPESCRIPT 2.7:
1 First of all, what does LVMH stand for?
2 Well, of course, it specialises in luxury products .... and it operates in a number of sectors.
3 Look at the brand names in each sector.
4 Each sector includes world-famous names.
5 Let's look first at wines and spirits.

3 This activity is an information exchange. You may want to demonstrate an exchange with two of your more able students. Divide the class into two groups; Group 1 finds out about Edizione Holding and Group 2 finds out about Sony. Both are holding companies. You will need to pre-teach *sectors* and *areas of business* and to point them out on both the Edizione chart and the Sony chart. Check that students understand that the colour coding represents sectors for Edizione. You might also need to help students to form the questions they will need to ask.

When the pairs are ready they should exchange information and complete the charts.

KEY:
Edizione Holding Family Tree
1 Benetton Group
2 Benetton Sportsystem
3 Benetton Formula
4 Gruppo GS
5 Autogrill
6 Edizione Property
7 Investimenti
8 Verdesport
9 Pallacanestro Treviso
10 Volley Treviso
11 Other minority interests

Sony
1 **Electronics** a Audio b Video c Televisions
d Info and Comm e Elec. comp.s
2 **Games** a Sony Computer Ent
b Games console and software
3 **Music** a Sony Music Ent. (Japan) inc.
4 **Pictures** a Sony Pictures Ent.
b Theatre Operations
5 **Insurance** a Sony Life Insurance Co.
6 **Other** a customer financing
b broadcasting

4 The students should now work with their partners to prepare a presentation on their holding company. Check they understand *overview*.

Final Task

Put a pair from Group 1 with a pair from Group 2 for the presentations. Monitor the presentations and give feedback and praise.

Checklist

1 Reuters / EMI / DHL / McDonald's / Granada Film / Pearson Plc – Financial Times Group / Virgin / Benetton / Mercedes-Benz / Sony / Edizione Holding
2 a Virgin = music retailing, Virgin Cola, radio, airline
b Sony = Electronics, games and music
c LVMH = wines and spirits, fashion and leather goods, fragrances and cosmetics
3 Food, music, manufacturing, farming, service industries, etc.
4 A parent company or one that owns others or subsidiaries
5 a present simple   b present continuous

Travel

Key Vocabulary

⬛ **3.1** You may like to use the cloze version of the Key Vocabulary (▶ page 94).

▶ **For more practice see Workbook page 10**

Lead-in

Students discuss the questions in pairs using the information in the picture. Tell them to keep a note of their answers for the next question. Get feedback from students, but don't give answers yet.

KEY:

1 She's in advertising (there's a copy of the advertising journal *Campaign* on her desk).
2 and 4 She's planning a trip to Poland (the schedule / air ticket is on her desk).
3 She's from the UK (her passport is visible).

Language Focus

1 ⬛ **3.2** Explain that the woman in the photo is Rosalind Harrison and that the students are now going to hear Mike Smith talking to her secretary. Play the tape once for the students to check if their guesses were correct, and direct attention to the clues in the photograph – see Key above.

TAPESCRIPT 3.2:

(**MS**= Mike Smith, **PG** = Pam García)
MS: Hello Pam. It's Mike, how are you?
PG: Oh hello Mike, I'm fine thanks, and you?
MS: Oh, not too bad. Could I speak to Rosalind Harrison?
PG: Oh, I'm sorry, Mike. I'm afraid she's out of the office at the moment – she's visiting a client in Manchester.
MS: Oh, OK. Well, maybe you can help. It's about the sales conference. Is she coming over to Warsaw next Tuesday?
PG: Yes, she's flying out on Monday morning, but she's visiting the Gdansk office first.
MS: So when is she coming to Warsaw then?
PG: I'm not sure, possibly on Tuesday, or she may spend another day in Gdansk and then go to Warsaw on Wednesday.
MS: OK, well I'm having a meeting with our Marketing Manager on Wednesday morning. That's at nine thirty. She's welcome to join in on that, and then I really *must* see her some time on Wednesday about the product launch.
PG: OK, I'll let her know.
MS: Thanks Pam. Hey, are you coming over with Rosalind?

PG: No, I'm not this time, but I *am* coming over in September!
MS: That's great, I'll look forward to seeing you! Bye for now!
PG: Bye.

2 Play the tape again for the students to answer the questions. Check answers as a class and write the full answers on the board. Elicit each time if it is a definite arrangement or only a suggestion. You may want to underline the verbs on the board and ask the class which tenses they are.

KEY:

1 a On Monday, Rosalind Harrison is flying to Gdansk.
  b On Wednesday, Mike Smith is having a meeting with his Marketing Manager.
  c In September, Pam is going over to Poland.
2 a All three arrangements are definite.
  b The present continuous (for definite future plans)

Pronunciation

⬛ **3.3**, **3.4** Play the tape, stopping after each contracted form for students to repeat.

Language Practice

1 Students match the verbs and nouns in preparation for the next exercise. Point out there is no indefinite article before *lunch* and *coffee*.

KEY:

1 Go on a tour	2 have lunch
3 have coffee	4 listen to a CD
5 have a meeting	6 listen to a presentation

3 One possible solution to the travel arrangements:

Dr Brook – He could take the Eurostar in the afternoon of the day of the dinner (he is starting from central London; it is cheap and convenient).
Ms Turner – She could travel by plane from Heathrow, staying overnight after the conference, or could go by car using Le Shuttle which is cheaper, and she could go and return the same day.
Mr Brown – He could travel by Stena Sealink.

Vocabulary One

1

KEY:

1 run a seminar (conduct a workshop)
2 hold a conference (give a talk?)
3 plan an itinerary (book a hotel)
4 book a ticket (first class seat)
5 throw a party (like to come?)
6 visit a subsidiary (arrange transport)
7 order a meal (join me?)

2 You might want to remind students about the language for offers which they studied in unit 2 before students do this exercise. If you think your students will need more help with this, write the following prompts up on the board (give a talk, join me etc). Check that students are using the present continuous for future plans and using the word partners correctly.

KEY: (The following are suggestions)

1 I'm running a seminar next month. Would you be able to conduct a workshop?

2 We're holding a conference in Paris next summer. Could you give a talk?

3 While we're planning the itinerary, would it be possible for you to book a hotel for us?

4 I'm booking my ticket this afternoon. Should I book a first class seat?

5 We're throwing a party on Saturday. Would you like to come?

6 If you're visiting the subsidiary on Tuesday, would you like me to arrange transport for you?

7 I'm going to order a meal for later. Shall I order for you too?

➤ **For more practice see Workbook page 10**

Writing

Draw students' attention to the fax at the bottom of the page. Focus on **Re:**. Ask 'What would you expect to see here?'. Elicit 'the subject of the fax'. Then ask students to have a look at the handwritten notes and give the fax a suitable title (e.g. Trip to Melbourne).

Listening

1 🔊 3.5 Before students listen to the interview, encourage them to read through the questions and think about possible answers. Check they understand what *jet lag* is.

Play the tape all the way through without pauses to encourage global listening skills.

TAPESCRIPT 3.5:

(**Int** = Interviewer, **CK** = Colin Knapp)

Int: Colin, do you travel on business very often?

CK: I travel to Thailand about two to three times per year.

Int: And how long is the flight from England to Thailand?

CK: The flight is about twelve hours.

Int: Uh, huh. Do you enjoy that long flight?

CK: It's, it is OK as long as I take plenty of reading, and they normally have three to four films.

CK: I watch all of the films because I find it very difficult to sleep on a, on a plane.

Int: OK. Do you erm suffer from jet lag after the flight?

CK: Er, I suffer jet lag, erm in Thailand it lasts for about one, one day.

Int: Uh, huh; and when you return to England?

CK: It is worse, for some reason, and is about three days.

Int: So travelling back to England is, is less pleasant?

CK: It is less pleasant, but that apparently is quite common.

Int: OK. Erm, and what's the reason for your visits to Thailand?

CK: It's to teach and to do some business with the University.

Int: Why do you need to travel there? Why can't you do business by telephone or fax?

CK: Because our discussions are quite complex and it ..., it is too complex for telephone and fax.

Int: OK. When you visit Thailand do you experience a culture gap?

CK: There is a culture gap, yes.

Int: Erm, and what are the ... can you give me any examples of that?

CK: They are very polite people, and so there are times when you may think they agree with you, but they are, they say yes because they think it is polite.

Int: OK. So the, the way people communicate is different?

CK: They communicate in a different way, yes.

Int: OK. And so can you give people visiting Thailand any tips, for their visit?

CK: Erm, always try to be polite, and be respectful, and on first meeting try not to look the person in the eye, erm too often.

KEY:

1 He travels two or three times per year.

2 He visits Thailand regularly.

3 The flight takes about twelve hours.

4 He reads and watches the films.

5 Yes, he does.

6 Yes, it is worse from east to west and takes three days to get over instead of one.

7 The discussions are too complex to have by telephone or fax.

8 Sometimes the Thais say yes to be polite, and not because they agree with you.

9 Try to be polite and respectful and try not to look the person in the eye too often.

2 Divide students into small groups to discuss the questions. If your students do not have much experience of international travel, you could replace some of the questions in the Students' Book with the following:

What's your favourite way of travelling? Why?

What do you like to do during a long journey?

If you have to travel a long way, what time of day do you prefer to travel? (e.g. early in the morning? overnight?)

What do you know about jet lag? etc. You could then use the rest of the questions in the book.

Reading

Discuss the theme of the article before reading to prepare the students for the text. Note the text is to be read in sections and the questions answered after each section.

1 Encourage students to read the questions in pairs or small groups.

2 Ask students to read through the questions before reading the first part of the text. Check that students understand *to be promoted*.

KEY:

1 12,000
2 Office lady
3 Yes, she does. She likes the parks and green fields.
4 She is on a scheme to give office ladies overseas experience.
5 She has no job opportunities in London; she cannot be promoted.
6 She is going back to Japan next year.
7 No, she doesn't, because there are few amusements and no opportunity to relax.

3 KEY:

1 Language difficulties and cultural differences.
2 Japanese dislike arguments and prefer majority opinions.

4 Ask students to discuss the question in pairs or small groups. Do they think it is easy for foreigners to meet people in their country?

Vocabulary Two

1 Before doing the exercise, check students can say their own nationality correctly and find out what languages they speak. Point out the examples where the stress pattern changes, e.g. Ja'pan – Japa'nese, 'China – Chi'nese, 'Portugal – Portu'guese.

KEY:

a Belgian	g Hungarian	m Mexican
b Brazilian	h Bahraini	n Polish
c British	i Irish	o Singaporean
d Canadian	j Omani	p Vietnamese
e Danish	k Italian	
f Finnish	l Maltese	

2 KEY:

1 French	3 Dutch	5 Thai
2 Greek	4 Swiss	

3 Students complete the exercise in pairs. Again, you might want to point out the changing stress pattern on 'Canada – Ca'nadian, 'Hungary – Hun'garian, 'Israel – Is'raeli, 'Italy – I'talian, 'Malta – Mal'tese, Viet'nam – Vietna'mese.

▶ **For more practice see Workbook page 11**

Cross-cultural Comparison

1 Check students understand *embrace* and *to be rude*. Encourage students to discuss their answers.

KEY:

a T	d T	g F	i F
b F	e T	h T	j T
c F	f F		

Note on c: It is important to keep the card visible and to show you have noticed the content and rank of the card's owner.

Once students have checked their answers, discuss whether they were surprised by any of the answers.

Business Communication

1 ▭ 3.6 Follow the activity as directed in the Students' Book.

TAPESCRIPT 3.6:

1 W: I'd like to introduce you to Señor Iglesias. Señor Iglesias this is Duncan Grove.
DG: Pleased to meet you.
SI : How do you do?

2 M: Do you know Caroline Courtney?
David/Caroline: No, hello.
David: Pleased to meet you. I'm David Walker.
Caroline: Nice to meet you.

3 SB: Hello, Ms Barty?
AB: Yes.
SB: I'm Stephen Brown.
AB: Oh, yes, hello. Nice to meet you. You work with Roslyn Davis, don't you?
SB: Yes, that's right.

4 M: Sofia, this is Barry. Barry, Sofia.
S: Hello, Barry. Nice to meet you.
B: Hello. Pleased to meet you.

5 M: Let me introduce Miss Kim. Miss Kim, this is Mr Kinzett.
Mr Kinzett: Pleased to meet you.
Miss Kim: Pleased to meet you.

6 J: Hi, I'm John.
F: Hello, my name's Fiona.

KEY:

1 Ms Kim – Mr Kinzett
2 Barry – Sofia
3 Caroline Courtney – David Walker
4 Stephen Brown – Ms Barty
5 Señor Iglesias – Duncan Grove
6 John Smith – Fiona

3 Demonstrate the task with one of the students. Introduce yourself then ask the student to respond.

4 3.7 In pairs, students discuss what they think the people are saying in each of the pictures. Play the tape for them to compare their answers.

TAPESCRIPT 3.7:

Colin:	Hello, how are you?
Michelle:	I'm fine thanks. How are you?
Colin:	Fine. It's nice to see you.
Michelle:	You too.
Colin:	Can I get you a drink?
Michelle:	Oh, yes thank you. I'll have a glass of wine please.
Colin:	Red or white?
Michelle:	White please.
Colin:	I'm afraid there's only red.
Michelle:	Oh, that's all right. Red's fine.
Colin:	Oh, I'm so sorry
Michelle:	That's all right, don't worry about it.
Colin:	I'm terribly sorry.
Michelle:	Really, it doesn't matter.

5 Play the tape again for students to complete the conversation. Stop the tape a couple of times to give students time to note down the missing words.

KEY: See tapescript 3.7

6 3.8 Students complete the conversation on their own or in pairs and listen to check their answers.

KEY:

1 d   2 b   3 c   4 a

TAPESCRIPT 3.8:

Roger:	Hello, Colin. Just to say the taxi will be here in a few minutes.
Colin:	Oh, Roger, let me introduce you to Michelle.
Roger:	Hello, Michelle. Nice to meet you.
Michelle:	Pleased to meet you. Sorry, I didn't catch your name.
Roger:	I'm Roger.
Colin:	We're having dinner at The Lemon Tree. Would you like to join us?
Michelle:	That's very kind of you. I'd love to, but I'm afraid I have to get home. My parents are coming to stay this weekend.
Colin:	Can we give you a lift?

Michelle:	Oh, that would be great. Thank you very much. I'll just get my coat.

7 3.9 Students should be able to answer the question after listening to the tape once. Play the tape again and stop after each phrase for students to check their answers.

TAPESCRIPT 3.9:

Michelle:	Thanks very much for the lift.
Colin:	Pleasure. Don't mention it.
Michelle:	Bye. Have a nice meal.
Roger:	Thanks very much. Have a good weekend.

KEY: They are in a taxi, **a, b, e, f**

8 Write the headings 'Thanks' and 'Apologies' on the board and elicit the different expressions. Drill the expressions for correct stress and intonation.

KEY: **1** apologies: Oh, that's all right
That's all right, don't worry about it.
Really, it doesn't matter.
2 thanks: (It's a) pleasure.
Don't mention it

► **For more practice see Workbook page 12**

Final Task

Before students do the roleplay, make sure they think through their holiday plans. Point out that this will form the basis of the conversation. Divide the students into groups of three. Make sure that students read through their cards and understand the situation. Tell the students that they should keep the conversation going for two to three minutes. When you clap your hands they should finish their conversations in a suitable way and say their good-byes. Listen to the students as they do the roleplay and note down any mistakes you hear.

Checklist:

1 a to talk about current activities or activities around the time of speaking
 b to talk about future arrangements
2, 3, 4, 5 Answers depend on students' choice; make sure they can explain why they made that choice.

Customers, Companies and Travel

The Review units are designed as a check on students' progress and a chance to consolidate learning. They are not formal tests and can be done in class. If you would like to test your students more formally, you will find four photocopiable tests in this Teacher's Book.

➤ **See page 32**

Business Review

Marks and Spencer is an international retailer, its products include food, clothes and household furnishings. The company is British and trains its staff to offer a friendly, professional service.

Kwik-Fit is a company which fits tyres and exhausts to cars. As its name suggests, the company offers a fast service, usually while the customer waits. It is a British company.

LVMH is a luxury goods group whose products include wines and spirits, fashion and leather goods and fragrances and cosmetics. It is a French company, and is committed to very high quality.

Sony is a Japanese company which manufactures electronic and hi-fi equipment. It also operates in the music sector and insurance.

McDonald's is the world's largest hamburger restaurant company. It is an American company and is committed to serving high quality food.

First Direct is a bank and offers a range of banking services. It is a British company and offers its customers 24-hour telephone banking.

Students work in pairs and discuss the questions. Alternatively, divide students into fours: Students A and B should be given three companies to discuss; Students C and D the other three companies. They should then change partners and describe the companies they have been discussing.

Vocabulary Review

1

Customers	Companies	Travel
1 repeat business	2 parent company	10 itinerary
4 code of practice	3 buying	11 colleagues
5 customer loyalty	12 subsidiaries	6 cultural
9 customer care	13 sector	difference
	14 selling	7 foreign
	15 marketing	business
	16 multinational	trip
	17 production	8 jet lag
		18 social
		conventions

You could ask your students to complete this task on OHT rather than in their books and then compare answers in class.

2 The definitions are all provided in the vocabulary sections of each unit. Encourage the students to look for them if they can't remember.

3 Accept any that are correct.
Encourage students to complete the exercise in pairs and take turns to give a definition for each word.

Grammar Review

Direct and indirect questions

1 Ask students to write the five questions on their own. Divide the class into As and Bs. Student A should ask student B the questions; Student B should give suitable answers. They should then change to work with another partner and Student B should ask the questions.

Accept any well-formulated questions in direct or indirect form, the following are examples:

1 Can you tell me what kind of experience trainees get?
2 Would you mind explaining about the work experience.
3 Are there any opportunities to specialise?
4 Can trainees choose where they get work experience?
5 Do trainees work on well-known newspapers?
6 Can you tell me if trainees work on well-known newspapers?
7 Is there any possibility of working for the company after the training course?
8 Could you tell me if there is any possibility of working for the company after the training course.

2 Divide students into groups of three. If there are any extra students they should take the same role as Student A. Make sure that students understand the situation. Give students A and B some time to think about what they are going to say and for Student C to think of the questions to ask. Help them as necessary.

Present simple and present continuous

3 Can the students recall the differences in form and function of the two tenses?

British Airways is an international airline which ¹carries over 28 million passengers each year. They ²are looking for graduates with potential for management.

SmithKline Beecham is a transnational healthcare company. SB ³is involved in research, development, production and marketing of healthcare products, and ⁴employs 54,000 people worldwide.

Aldi is a large, international food retailer. It ⁵has over 100 stores in the UK, and ⁶is opening many new stores.

Writing and Business Communication Review

1 Direct attention to the picture at the bottom of the page. It shows a Boeing 747 in a hanger. Ask the students to read the text and answer the questions.

1 Boeing is an aerospace company which manufactures aircraft.
2 Boeing manufactures civil aircraft, military aeroplanes and develops advanced computer technology.
3 The company is based in Seattle, Washington and is American.

2

The Boeing company is an enormous American aerospace company which manufactures aircraft. Over 400 airlines use them. The company manufactures civil aircraft and military aeroplanes and develops advanced computer technology. The US Government buys its military planes, systems and space vehicles from them.

Boeing's headquarters are in Seattle, Washington State. 87,000 people work for the company there. Over 116,000 work directly for the company in the USA and Canada. 60% of their sales are overseas.

3 The students can give their short presentations in pairs or groups.

Reading

- **Look at questions 1–5.**
- **For each question, which sentence is correct, a, b or c?**

1

> ALL VISITORS MUST REPORT TO THE
> OFFICE TO COLLECT SAFETY CLOTHING.

a   At the office visitors will get a report.
b   At the office visitors will get special clothes.
c   At the office visitors will get instructions.

2

> Exports:
> 1997 – £3.78M, 1998 – £7.79M, 1999 – £5.64M

a   Exports went up in the period 1997-1999.
b   Exports decrease in the period 1997-1999.
c   1998 was a bad year for exports.

3

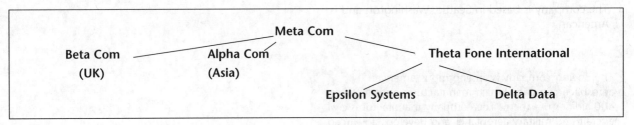

a   Meta Com is a subsidiary company.
b   Beta Com is an international company.
c   Theta Fone International is a parent company.

4

> All new staff are invited to attend a reception on 24th
> May at 7.45p.m. in room 579. Please reply to room 136.

a   The reception is for all staff.
b   The reception is at a quarter to eight in the evening.
c   The reception is in room 136.

5

> The computer help desk is closed today for a staff
> seminar. In an emergency call extension 3579.

a   Anyone with a serious problem should go to the seminar.
b   Anyone with a serious problem should call 3579.
c   Anyone with a serious problem should come back tomorrow.

Speaking

Candidate A

You need to ask Candidate B for this information about a hotel.

Your Questions

Address _____

Name of Manager _____ E-mail address _____

Conference room? _____ Restaurant facilities _____

Your Information

Hotel Tartan
35 Westgate Street, Edinburgh
Manager: M MacIntosh

tel/fax: 0131 682 2772	*Single and double rooms*
e-mail: Hottartan.com.uk	*all with bathrooms ensuite*
Bar	*Gymnasium*
Restaurant	*Swimming pool*
Conference room	*Car hire*

✂ •

Speaking

Candidate B

You need to ask Candidate A for this information about a hotel.

Your Questions

Location _____

Fax Number _____ Car hire _____

Restaurant facilities _____ Conference room _____

Your Information

Hotel Eurostar
346 Park Street, London W4
Manager: M MacIntosh

tel: 0207-456 3288	*Single and double rooms*
e-mail: Hoteurostar.co.uk	*all with bathrooms ensuite*
Bar	*Gymnasium*
Restaurant	*Swimming pool*
Conference room	*Car hire*

Writing

Read the memo and the leaflet, then complete the form.

WISLEY MEMO

To: Sharon Swaine
From: Sandy Carter, Office Manager
Date: 14 May 2000
Re: Office Chairs

We decided at the last departmental meeting that all administrative workers need new chairs.
This is a great opportunity to get a good product at a good price.
Please order 6 chairs for the reception area.

Thanks

Special Offer

Buy 2 or more Siteasy office chairs and get a third one **FREE!!**

Order your Siteasy office chairs within the next 4 weeks and take advantage of this great offer.
Hurry while stocks last.

Siteasy office chairs – £19.99 each or 3 for £39.98. £12.50 delivery charge on all orders.

WISLEY PURCHASE ORDER

QUANTITY	PRODUCT REQUIRED	PRICE	POSTAGE AND PACKING
		£_____ each £_____ for 3	£
		TOTAL	**£**

Listening

For questions 1 and 2 you will hear two short recordings.
For each question, mark A, B or C for the most suitable answer.

Question 1
Where would Mr Gawlinski like to go after the conference?

a   museum

b   theatre

c   cinema

Question 2
Which is the correct platform for the train to London?

a   Platform 6

b   Platform10

c   Platform 5

Question 3

• **Look at the notes below.**

• **You will hear a manager discussing the contents of a brochure with her assistant.**

• **Listen to the conversation and write in the missing numbers.**

• **You will hear the conversation twice.**

Changes to make to the sports centre brochure:

opening date (1) _____ December

number of tennis courts (2) _____

length of swimming pool (3) ._____

number of brochures to print (4) _____

---

unit 4

Troubleshooting

Further information about Ford is available at:

Ford: http://www.ford.com

Key Vocabulary

🎞 **4.1** To introduce the subject, ask students to look at the title of the unit and tell you what they think it means (*dealing with difficult problems*). Ask if they can work out what a person is called who goes into a company to help with specific problems (*troubleshooter*).

Read this section through with the students. Make sure that the students can pronounce as well as use the key words by playing the recorded version. It may be useful to ask the students for the goals/strategy of any business that they are familiar with.

You may like to use the cloze version of the Key Vocabulary text. (▶ page 94)

▶ **For more practice see Workbook page 16**

Lead-in

1 The text is about an agency for fashion models. Ask students to name any high-profile fashion models they know.

KEY:

1	reputation	2	Jonathan Phang (new MD)
3	models from other agencies	4	costs
5	profits	6	who aren't making money
7	excellent models	8	clients
		9	money

2 To demonstrate the task, go through the first few points with the students and then ask students to continue in pairs.

3 Students change partners to see if they agree on the SWOT analysis. Point out that there is no one correct answer.

NOTE
SWOT analysis is a tool which helps to monitor how well a company is doing within its economic environment. It assesses performance not just in the company's own terms, but against other similar firms. The information helps managers plan and make strategic decisions about the future of the company.

The following is a *suggestion* for the SWOT. Other variants are possible. Often a weakness (such as low profits) can be viewed as an opportunity (e.g. to improve sales); a strength (such as being a market leader) could offer a threat (e.g. of take-over); and a strength (such as an MD with a lot of experience) can

be an opportunity (e.g. to expand the business), etc. Accept anything that the students can justify successfully.

Strengths
In the past – one of the best known companies.
New MD has a lot of experience.

Weaknesses
IMG no longer has a reputation for being a fashionable, forward-looking company.
IMG has models on their books who are not earning money for the company.

Opportunities
IMG is looking for new models.
MD has ability to make good financial decisions.
Models switch to good agencies quickly.
Profits can be excellent for a successful company.

Threats
Model agency business is very competitive.
All model agencies are looking for new models.

Language Focus

Should and *ought to*: making recommendations

1 🎞 **4.2**
NOTE Play the tape through without pauses, but be prepared to replay it. The people on the tape talk about 'soft selling' and 'hard selling'. These are two approaches that a salesperson might adopt. The 'hard' sell is one where the salesperson takes the lead and is aggressive or 'pushy' towards the customer. With 'soft' selling the salesperson still wants to sell the goods but is less aggressive and allows the customer to feel that he/she is making all the decisions.

TAPESCRIPT 4.2:

(**AB** = Anna Brook, **BW** = Belinda Waters)

AB: I don't think car manufacturers and car dealers think about female customers at all.
BW: I know what you mean. Car dealers don't seem to listen to what women say they want.
AB: Yes, they should take us seriously. After all, women are buying more cars these days.
BW: Yes, so they should have more women selling cars.
AB: Mm. The dealers are nearly always men and they do such a hard sell. I think they ought to use a soft-sell approach.
BW: I agree. I really don't like the hard sell. You know, I also think things like children's car seats and car phones should be available as standard.
AB: Yes definitely, why don't they fit car phones in all new cars? Women on their own feel much safer with a phone in the car.
BW: And they should change the adverts too, I think.
AB: Yes, I think there should be lots of product

36

information in adverts. They ought to tell us about things like petrol consumption and safety features.

BW: I hate these adverts just showing us fast cars in exotic locations.

AB: Me too.

KEY:

1 d   2 a   3 c   4 b   5 e

2 Play the tape again for students to complete the sentences. You may want to stop the tape a few times to give students time to complete the notes.

KEY:

1 a should take	3 a should change
b should have	b should be
c ought to use	c ought to tell
2 should be	

3 Copy one of the recommendations with *should* and one of the recommendations with *ought to* on the board and highlight the verb which follows. Students complete the exercise in pairs and check their answers with the Grammar Reference on page 153.

NOTE You might want to point out to students that we tend to use *should* in the negative and question form rather than *ought to*.

KEY:

1b infinitive without *to*
2a They shouldn't listen to women.
 b They ought not to include car phones in all new cars.

Pronunciation

🔲 4.3, 4.4:

1 Play the tape and repeat enough times so students hear the falling intonation.

2 You might like to model these sentences for the students using backchaining – start with the final word, students repeat, then the last two words and so on to build up an accurate pattern of intonation.

Language Practice

1 Students complete the matching exercise on their own and check answers with a partner. One person reads out the situation and their partner reads out the correct solution. Check students can pronounce *repu'tation* and *com'petitive*.

KEY:

1 e   2 c   3 d   4 b   5 a

2 Students can complete the quiz on their own or you could go through the advice as a class to make

sure that students understand the points that are being made. Make sure students answer with what they actually *do* rather than what they think they should do. After completing the quiz, the prompts could be used for a transformation task. For each sentence, ask students to write a 'should' sentence, e.g. 1 *You shouldn't avoid a problem, you should deal with it.*

3 Encourage students to discuss their answers with a partner and give each other advice on how to deal with problems.

▶ **For more practice see Workbook page 17**

Reading

1 Remind students of the points that the two women made about the way that companies sell cars in the Listening passage. Find out what your students think. Do they agree with what the two women said? Do they think different sales techniques should be used for men and women? Then read the first paragraph of the reading passage to see which of the points the writer also makes.

KEY:

1 The writer focuses on:
c Car manufacturers and dealers should take women buyers seriously and think about the different needs of male/female buyers.
 We can infer that the writer would probably agree with the other two points the women made.

2 Direct the students to read the whole article now, then complete the summary. Students should check answers in pairs.

KEY:

1 spy		2 Women's Marketing Panel
3 16		4 women Ford workers
5 9		6 their products and service
7 4		8 10
9 reports		10 senior management

▶ **For more practice, there is another reading in the Workbook, page 17**

Vocabulary

Synonyms

1 Highlight the different expressions that are used for Ford in the text. Ask students why they think the different expressions are used (e.g. *to avoid repeating the same expression, to make the text more interesting*). Students match the synonyms and compare answers in pairs.

KEY:

1 c	2 d	3 a	4 b

Word building

2 Students complete the table. Encourage them to mark which part of the word is stressed.

KEY:

NOUN	VERB
a 'buyer	to buy
an 'increase	to in'crease
a 'product	to pro'duce
partici'pation	to par'ticipate
a 'visit	to 'visit
a recommen'dation	to recomm'end

3 Ask students to read their sentences to the class to check for meaning and correct pronunciation.

Writing

Clauses of purpose

1 Lead into the subject by asking students why they do different things, e.g. *Why are you studying English?* Use one of the answers as an example and write it up on the board and highlight the clause of purpose.

KEY:

1 b	2 a	3 c

2 Students complete the exercises on their own or in pairs. Encourage them to use all three patterns.

KEY:

1 d	3 b	5 e	7 f
2 c	4 a	6 g	

3 Students complete the exercises on their own or in pairs. Encourage them to use all three patterns.

KEY:

1 see example.
2 We are having a meeting (in order) to discuss the problems with sales.
3 Ford is sending in 'spies' (in order) to get information about dealers.
4 The consultant is visiting in order to make recommendations.
5 The company is changing its advertising so that more women buy its products.
6 I am planning for next year now so that I can anticipate any problems and try to prevent them.
7 We are asking the models to leave so as to make the company more profitable.

4 Students take it in turns to ask and answer the questions. For information on the correct layout of a report see Workbook page 69.

➤ **For more practice of these clauses see Workbook page 18**

Listening

1 📼 **4.5** Encourage students to discuss the questions in pairs or small groups.

TAPESCRIPT 4.5:

(**Int** = Interviewer, **M** = Manager)

Int: Why do you think troubleshooting, or solving problems, is so important in business?

M: Well these days, erm, business is extremely competitive and it's competitive in terms of time and in terms of money. Whenever a company tries to compete with another company, it tries to get a new product out quickly and it tries to do it without spending too much money. Problems, when they arise, cost money and they waste time.

Int: And, are there any particular areas which are typical trouble spots?

M: Starting at the very beginning of a project, quite often people don't plan effectively. You can never plan early enough, especially in a large and complex project. Part of that planning involves making sure that everybody on the project understands his or her role; and that the objectives of the project are regularly reviewed, so that everybody understands how the project is going to meet the needs of the market, and whether it is still relevant.

Int: Do you think that, erm everyone has a role in troubleshooting and anticipating problems, or do you see it as only a managerial skill?

M: I think it can quite often happen that managers start a project, think it's going very well, walk away from it and then are very surprised six months later when it's going wrong. Er, everybody, at whatever level, should make sure that they ask the right questions, and indeed try to, as you say, anticipate problems and raise those problems with their managers and with their colleagues at regular review intervals.

Int: Do you have any other tips for solving problems?

M: It's very important that a project team communicates well within itself and also to people outside the team. You should try to have a democratic spirit in a project, allowing people to speak openly, to ask questions and to feel that they own the project as much as the managers or the client may do.

Int: What's the one most important strategy to avoid problems?

M: In my opinion, in order to avoid problems happening you should be realistic. You should be realistic in the number of people working on the project, the cost of the project and the size of the project. When you put pressure on a project because you don't have enough people working on it, or you are spending too much money, you create problems. Pressure means problems, so to avoid problems, reduce the pressure.

2 Tell students not to worry about understanding every word, but to focus on the information they need to complete the gaps.

KEY:

1 Business is competitive in terms of *time* and *money*.
2 Problems can *cost* money and *waste* time.
3 At the beginning of a project often people don't *plan effectively*.
4 Planning helps to make sure that everybody *understands his or her role*.
5 In a project, everybody should make sure that they *ask the right questions* and *anticipate problems*.
6 It's important that a project team *communicates* well.
7 You should try to have a *democratic* spirit in a project.
8 In order to avoid problems you should be *realistic* about the number of people working on the project, the *cost* and the *size* of the project.
9 When you put pressure on a project you *create problems*.

3 Encourage students to discuss their initial thoughts about what the manager said. If your students are already working, ask them if they agree with the manager. Then play the tape again.

Business Communication

2 Divide students into pairs. Student A should describe the problems and answer any questions that Student B has. They should decide together which are the areas that are most important.

3 In the same pairs, students should decide on a recommendation for each point and then complete the recommendation section of the report in 4. Remind students to use the clauses of purpose.

4 Note: if you think your students will be inhibited about commenting on their partner's work, you could just discuss the exercise with them.

Final Task

Encourage students to describe the problems and add any other details they want rather than just reading the situations out.

Student A

Your partner is a colleague. Ask for his/her help with the following situations:

1 Your customers are moving to your competitor because their prices are low.

2 A new overseas customer is coming to visit your company for the first time.

3 One of your members of staff is working until very late every evening.

4 A new product is not selling well. You think there may be a design fault.

Now offer your partner some help with his/her problems.

Student B

You are a colleague of Student A. Your partner is asking you for help with some situations. Make recommendations and/or offer solutions.

Now ask your partner for help with the following situations.

1 Your colleague is preparing a presentation to a group of prospective new clients.

2 Your company, based in Europe, is opening a branch in Brazil.

3 The computers in the sales department are out of date.

4 The number of customer complaints is increasing.

Checklist

1 'solving problems'
2 plan carefully – particularly time and resources, and be realistic
3 SWOT
4 *Should* and *Ought to*
5 (Make sure students use the clause of purpose correctly.)

Company History

Further information about some of the companies mentioned in this unit is available at these websites:

> Marks and Spencer: http://www.marks-and-spencer.com
> Doctor Marten: http://drmarten.com

If your students have access to the Internet, you could ask them to do research from the company websites.

Key Vocabulary

5.1 If your students are already working, ask them what they know about their company's history. You may need to give them some prompts: *Who? When? Where?* etc.

You may like to use the cloze version of the Key Vocabulary. (➤ page 94) You could give it to your students to see how many of the words they know before beginning the unit.

➤ **For more practice see Workbook page 19**

Lead-in

This is a useful place to teach your students how to say years, e.g.
1968 – nineteen sixty-eight
1911 – nineteen eleven
2005 – two thousand and five

1 Find out what students can remember about Marks and Spencer from Unit 1. Ask them to look at the pictures of important events in its history and discuss in pairs what they think the pictures show and when each event happened.

2 **5.2** Play the tape for students to note down the date. Check answers by students giving the year and describing what is shown in the photo.

TAPESCRIPT 5.2:

> In 1894 Michael Marks and Tom Spencer formed a partnership.
>
> In 1928 they registered the St Michael trademark.
>
> In 1930 the company opened the Marble Arch store on Oxford Street in London.
>
> In 1931 they introduced canned goods such as tomato soup.
>
> In 1975 Marks and Spencer opened stores in Paris and Brussels.
>
> In 1988 they opened two stores in Hong Kong.
>
> In 1997 they won the Queen's award for Export Achievement for the fifth time.

KEY:

a Marks and Spencer formed a partnership, 1894.
b They opened stores in Paris and Brussels, 1975.
c The company opened the Marble Arch store in London, 1930.
d They opened two stores in Hong Kong, 1988.
e They won the Queen's award for Export Achievement, 1997.

Language Focus

Past simple: regular and irregular verbs

1 Before reading, remind students that they came across Ford in unit 4. What can they remember about it?

COMPANY NOTE Students might be interested to know that Ford bought Volvo in January 1999.

2 Ask students to give full answers to check that they can pronounce the years correctly.

KEY:

1896 – he built his first car
1903 – he formed the Ford Motor Company
12 – the number of local businessmen who backed him
1911 – his first UK assembly plant opened
1929 – started to build a plant in Dagenham
1931 – the first Model AA truck rolled off the production line

3 and **4** Students complete the sentences and use their answers to work through the focus on the past simple.

KEY:

3
1 built   3 backed   5 started
2 formed   4 opened

4
1 by adding -ed to the infinitive.
2 build – built
3 a When <u>did</u> it all <u>start</u>?
  b When <u>did</u> it <u>come</u> to Britain?
4 a Ford built the first car in 1896, but he <u>didn't</u> <u>form</u> the company until 1903.
  b The first truck <u>didn't</u> <u>roll off</u> the line until 1931.

Pronunciation

1 **5.3** Highlight the pronunciation of the different endings on the board and play the cassette for students to hear the pronunciation.

2 **5.4** Play the sentences on the tape, pausing so students have time to repeat them.

TAPESCRIPT 5.4:

1 He formed a company.
2 They started making cars.
3 They stopped making Model B trucks.

3 Students can practise saying the verbs in Language Focus exercise 3 in pairs.

► **For more practice see Workbook page 19**

Language Practice

1 Ask if students own or have ever owned a pair of Doc Marten shoes. Find out if they know anything about the company history: *Who invented them? When? What nationality is the company? Why do you think they are popular?* Ask students to read the text to see if they can find the answers to any of these questions.

2 and **3** Students note down the past simple forms of the verbs. Ask them to read out their answers and check for correct pronunciation of the -*ed* endings.

KEY:

went (irregular), made (irregular), patented, developed, sold (irregular), went (irregular), adopted, wore (irregular), came (irregular), set up (irregular), became (irregular), offered, liked

4 Students ask and answer questions based on the text. This could be done as a memory game.

5 [cassette] 5.5 Students complete the questions before they listen and check their questions are correct by listening to the tape.

KEY:

1 When did you buy (your first pair of Doc Martens) them?
2 How much did they cost?
3 Where did you buy them?
4 What colour were they?
5 Why did you buy them (did you choose Doc Martens)?
6 Do you still wear Doc Martens?

6 Play the tape again with pauses so students have time to note down the answers she gives.

TAPESCRIPT 5.5:

(**Int** = Interviewer, **FW** = Faith Walker)

Int: When did you buy your first pair of Doc Martens?
FW: When I was 24 – that was in 1987.
Int: How much did they cost then?
FW: Erm, at that time they cost £25.00.
Int: Where did you buy them?
FW: I bought them in London, in Oxford Street.

Int: What colour were they?
FW: They were cherry red.
Int: Why did you choose Doc Martens?
FW: Well, because they were very fashionable in the 80s and I liked the style.
Int: Do you still wear Doc Martens?
FW: Yes, I still like the style.

KEY:

1 When I was 24, in 1987.
2 They cost £25.
3 I bought them in London.
4 They were cherry red.
5 Because they were fashionable and I liked the style.
6 Yes, I still like the style.

► **For more Language Practice see Workbook page 20**

Reading

1 Ask students to think of three products produced by Bic. Check that they understand the word *disposable*. They should look at the text very quickly to see if the products they thought of are mentioned.

2 Discuss in pairs or as a class.

3 Before completing this exercise, point out that the vocabulary is glossed.

KEY:

Company history
1950   The company was founded.
1950–53 Lazlo Biro invented the first pen.
        Marcel Bich [1]*refined* and [2]*modified* the design.
        Bich negotiated with Biro to [3]*produce and sell* the pen.
1953   Production of the [4]*Bic 'Crystal'* began.
1956   Sales of the biro rose to [5]*a quarter of a million a day*.
1972   Bic invented [6]*the disposable lighter.*
1975   Bic invented [7]*the throwaway razor.*
Now   Bic sells [8]*20 million* ball point pens per day.
        Bic sells [9]*4 million* disposable lighters per day.
        Bic and [10]*Gillette* are leaders in the market for disposable razors.

Vocabulary

1 Draw students' attention to the example household name and ask them to explain what they think it means. Can they think of any other examples of household names? Students complete the matching exercise in pairs.

KEY:

1 f	2 a	3 b
4 e	5 d	6 c

2 Do the first one as an example. Write the word 'object' on the board and elicit which adjectives in the list in exercise 1 can be used with it (*household, everyday*). Students do the same with the other nouns.

KEY:

The following are common collocations, there may be other possibilities:
a household object, everyday object
b disposable lighter
c competing companies
d healthy competition
e product development, healthy development

The Cross-cultural Comparison can be done as a discussion exercise in pairs/groups and possibly written up afterwards.

► **For more practice of some of this vocabulary see Workbook page 19**

Cross-cultural Comparison

In a multinational class, try and organise students into groups with as many different nationalities as possible. In a monolingual class, encourage students to compare their own country with another one which they know well.

Writing

1 Ask students in pairs to order the products.

KEY:

1 Biro	2 lighter	3 razor
4 windsurfing board		

2 Students read the passage to check their answers to exercise 1.

3 Divide students into pairs. Student Bs should look at their information on page 147. Monitor the students as they do the exercise and note down any problems with the past simple question formation and the pronunciation of the *-ed* endings.

NOTE LP stands for long playing record and describes a 33 rpm record. Vinyl records pre-date CDs.

KEY:

Date	Event
1948	EMI introduced long playing vinyl records (LPs).
1952	EMI producedd 45 rpm vinyl singles.
1958	EMI introduced stereophonic LP records.
1966	EMI introduced the first recording on cassette.
1983	EMI launched its first compact discs.
1994	EMI invested in VIVA, a music video channel.
Today	One of the world's leading music companies.

4 This can be done as a collaborative task in pairs.

► **For more practice on sequencing ideas see Workbook page 21**

Listening

1 Students match the terms with the definitions. Point out that these terms are all used in the Listening passage.

KEY:

1 asset management; **b** a company gives you financial advice, then manages your possessions.
2 insurance; **a** paying a sum of money (a premium) to a company to take on a risk for you.
3 re-insurance; **d** an insurance company buys its own insurance from other insurance companies, to share the risk of loss.
4 to merge; **c** to join together to form a new company (though one usually has the leading share).

2 ▭ 5.6a This is the first section of the Pat Woodgate interview. Play the cassette though without pausing, but be prepared to re-play it at least once more.

TAPESCRIPT 5.6a:

Pat Woodgate: Hello. I'm going to talk to you today about the key developments in the history of the company I work for and then tell you about the company's current position.

I am based in the Loss Control Department of Zurich Municipal which is part of the Zurich Financial Services Group. Zurich Municipal is a strategic business unit dealing solely with the public sector, e.g. local government, national health trusts, etc.

The company began its history when Zurich Insurance Company was founded 125 years ago in Zurich, Switzerland under the name of Versicherungs-Verein, or Insurance Association.

Unit 5 *Company History* ■

KEY:

1a the key developments in the history of the company
 b the company's current position
2a Pat works in the Loss Control Department of *Zurich Municipal*, part of the Zurich *Financial Services* Group.
 b The company deals with the public sector e.g. local government and national health trusts.
3 The company was founded in Zurich, Switzerland.
4 Insurance Association

3 ⬛ 5.6b

TAPESCRIPT 5.6b:

Pat Woodgate: They started business in May 1873, initially providing re-insurance – that is where they provide insurance cover to other insurance companies so that the risk is distributed throughout the market. They quickly entered into the field of accident insurance and obtained licences to conduct business in other European countries in 1875.

In 1922 the Zurich Insurance Company opened for business in the UK, with London-based headquarters. After many years of increased growth, in 1993 they took over the business of Municipal Mutual Insurance, who were the previous market leaders in providing insurance to the public sector.

In September 1998 the Zurich Insurance Company merged with British American Financial Services, that is the financial services operation of British American Tobacco Industries, thus forming Zurich Financial Services Group.

The group now has over 68,000 employees and over 30 million customers in over 50 countries. It is one of the ten largest companies worldwide, offering insurance and asset management.

KEY:

1 e 1998   **4 a** 1873
2 b 1875   **5 d** 1993
3 c 1922

4 KEY:

Employees: ¹*over 68,000 employees*
Customers: ²*30 million customers*
Countries: ³*over 50 countries*
Status of company: ⁴*insurance and asset management*.

Business Communication

1 Divide students into an even number of groups with a maximum of four students per group. (In the following exercise students will give their presentations to a student from a different group.) Draw the students' attention to the guidelines for giving presentations. It might be an idea to give students an example presentation to show them what you expect. If you wish, suggest students check the

company's website for further information and for suitable graphics to use for the presentation.

If students are preparing the presentation in class, give them a clear indication of how much time they have to prepare their presentations and suggest that they practise it in their groups before doing it for real. Give ample time for the presentation.

2 Pair up students from different groups for their presentations. Make sure that the students give each other feedback on their presentations. If you have a small class, the presentations could be videoed.

Final Task

Students could also include extra information by checking the company website.

Checklist

2 make – made, develop – developed, build – built, sell – sold, go – went
3 biro, disposable lighters and razors, windsurfing boards
4 verb endings: **a**/t/ **b**/t/ **c**/d/ **d**/d/ **e**/ɪd/ **f**/ɪd/

43

Retailing

Further information about the company discussed in this unit is available at this website:

Ikea: www.ikea.com

If your students have access to the Internet, you could ask them to do research from the company website.

Key Vocabulary

🎧 **6.1** Read through the Key Vocabulary with the students. Make sure that they can pronounce as well as use the words by playing the recorded version.

It may help to ask them to provide examples of a manufacturer, wholesaler and retailer. Do they use the Internet, TV shopping channels or catalogues? What are the advantages of these methods of shopping?

You may like to use the cloze version of the key vocabulary. (► page 94) You could give it to your students to see how many of the key words they know before beginning the unit.

► **For more practice see Workbook page 22**

Lead-in

Before the lead-in activity, ask students to predict what they think are the most common reasons for not liking shopping. When they have done this direct their attention to the graph on page 56.

1 KEY:
1 The two main reasons why people don't like shopping are queues and crowds.
2 Retailers can, for example, open longer hours, offer a delivery service, make sure more sales staff are available, offer home shopping facilities (e.g. catalogues, Internet), set up order lines (customers order over the phone and collect from the store)

Vocabulary One

Before you start, check sudents remember the difference between 'Retail Sales' and 'Direct Sales'. Make sure the students practise the vocabulary in the discussion activities.

NOTE *Shop* and *store* are synonyms, though *store* is an American term.

1

KEY:

Retail Outlet	Definition
1 supermarket	d a large self-service shop selling food and drink and also small household items
2 hypermarket	a a very large supermarket often located on the edge of a town or city
3 shopping centre/mall	e a covered area with shops, supermarkets and restaurants
4 department store	c a large shop with many departments or sections – each department sells a different type of goods.
5 specialist retailer	f a shop which only sells one type of product, usually of high quality
6 chain store	b one of a group of shops owned by the same company

4 When students have matched the definitions, ask them if they use any of these methods of shopping and what they buy. Ask them to give you the names of mail order catalogues, TV shopping channels and Internet sites they know. This could be a lead-in to the cross-cultural comparison.

KEY:

Direct sales	Definition
1 mail order	b a company sends goods by post from its warehouse
2 door-to-door sales	d an agent for the company sells the product or service to the customer at home
3 TV sales	c customers see product adverts on the screen and place their orders by phone/fax/the Internet
4 The Internet (e-commerce)	e electronic shopping from companies' websites
5 cash and carry	a customers can buy from the manufacturer's warehouse

Language Focus One

NOTE Ø This symbol means that no article is needed (the so-called 'zero' article).

1 First check students' understanding of the terms *countable* and *uncountable* by asking about everyday objects and things. Then ask students to put the words form the box into two lists – countable and uncountable. The abstract nouns are all uncountable.

KEY:

Countable: consumer product computer shop
Uncountable: information entertainment protection shopping advice

2 You will need to talk through the example sentences with the students, explaining the terms in italics. Point out/ask how the article is used in each case.

KEY:

1 single countable nouns referred to for the first time = *a/an*
2 plural countable nouns referred to for the first time = Ø
3 uncountable nouns = Ø
4 something already referred to or understood = the

Pronunciation

[cassette] **6.2** Tell students that *the* is pronounced differently depending on emphasis and position. Play the sentences twice – first time for students to identify the sounds and then to repeat them in context. Once they have identified the sounds, you could write the phonetic symbols on the board.

KEY:

1 /ðə/   2 /ði:/   3 /ði:/

Language Practice

1 Pre-teach *household* and *on-line*. When you check students answers, ask them which article is used for each type of noun.

KEY:

1 countable … countable	5 uncountable … countable
2 countable	6 countable … uncountable
3 countable	7 countable … countable
4 uncountable	

2 To contextualise the text in question 2, it is important that the students discuss the need for protection before reading it. This exercise may provide a good opportunity to do some work on the Internet. You could try a search on 'home shopping' to see what comes up. The range of sites might reveal some advantages and disadvantages/problems such as 'Which site should I choose?' and 'Is it reputable?'

KEY:

Protection for customers using the Internet is necessary because there is almost no consumer protection for electronic payment systems. There are problems of security of payment (e.g. other people using your passwords or code) and privacy of information (e.g. bank account or credit card details) and fraud (theft) is common.

3 KEY:

Advantages: convenience
Disadvantages: lack of consumer protection and privacy of information

4 KEY:

1 Ø	4 a	7 Ø	10 Ø
2 a	5 an	8 a	11 the
3 a	6 Ø	9 the	12 the

➡ **For more practice see Workbook page 23**

Reading

These activities practise both scan reading and detailed reading. It may be worth pointing this out again to students, and showing them how an initial scan can make it easier to understand a text by giving a sense of the whole. A good way to scan is to read the first sentence of each paragraph. Another way is to read the opening and closing paragraphs in a text.

1 Direct the students to the subheading only.

KEY:

The price

2 Ask students to look through the text very quickly. Detailed and careful reading is required for questions 3 and 4 only.

KEY:

The country in which the product was registered, manufacturer's or supplier's code, product and package size.

3 KEY:

1 978 the code for a book or magazine
2 05823 manufacturer/supplier's code
3 3439 product/package size
4 6 check digit

4 KEY:

13 – number of digits in a barcode
50 – the country code for the UK and Ireland
880 – the country code for South Korea
00183 – the manufacturer's code for Cadbury

Vocabulary Two

1 KEY:

1 checkout counter	5 supplier
2 barcode	6 packaging
3 manufacturer	7 price
4 till display	8 stock

2 This exercise could provide you with a good opportunity to practise the unstressed pronunciation of *of* /əv/.

KEY:

1 carton of milk	6 tin of tuna fish
2 bag of crisps	7 box of chocolates
3 packet of cigarettes/crisps	8 tub of margarine
4 can of cola	9 jar of jam
5 bottle of wine	10 bar of chocolate

3 KEY:

Uncountable: milk, margarine, Cola, wine, chocolate, jam

Listening

1 ▭ **6.3** Direct the students to the brief discussion before they listen. Have any of them ever been to an IKEA store?

2 Play the tape through without pauses, but be prepared to replay it once.

TAPESCRIPT 6.3:

(**Int** = Interviewer, **SR** = Sarah Rochford)

Int: How often do you visit an IKEA store?

SR: I probably visit the store about twice a year. I keep the erm catalogue at home and look through that during the year, and then make a visit about twice a year.

Int: What do you think of their products?

SR: I think they have a very good range of products, erm, I'm impressed with the quality of them; you get good quality for the price that you pay, and additionally I think that most of the products are environmentally sound.

Int: How about the stores – do you like them?

SR: Well, it's nice to try out the products, to be able to see them and try them out, and the layout of the store is very nice, erm, they do have a good selection of household accessories in the Marketplace, erm, and it's very easy for people with children – they have a playroom and pushchairs and suchlike.

Int: What type of things do you buy at IKEA?

SR: Well, I usually buy functional items such as bookcases and lamps and things like that, and then sometimes I buy textiles and bed linen.

Int: Are there any aspects of shopping at IKEA that you don't like?

SR: Oh there are! erm, it can be very crowded because it's a popular store, you can get a lot of people. This results often in very long queues at the check-outs; you can wait for quite a long time to pay for your goods, so that's my main problem with shopping there.

Int: So are you planning another trip to IKEA?

SR: Yes, I expect so. I'll probably go again in January for the sales.

KEY:

1 about twice per year
2 very good range of products, good quality, environmentally sound
3 nice to try out the products and see them, layout of stores is very good, easy for people with children
4 functional items (e.g. bookcases, lamps), textiles and bed linen
5 very crowded, long queues at the checkouts
6 January – for the sales (all shops in the UK hold sales in early January)

After listening direct the students to question 3.

Language Focus Two

1 Read through the examples with the students and point out the noun and how it is connected to the information.

2 ▭ **6.4** Play the cassette once through, then replay if necessary.

TAPESCRIPT 6.4:

One: I prefer sales assistants who let me look around by
    myself.

Two: I think it's important to have packaging that clearly shows the ingredients.

Three: Because of the children, I need shops which have car parks.

Four: I like shops that offer a wide variety of goods.

Five: I like shopping malls where all my favourite shops are in one place.

Six: I don't like door-to-door salespeople who put you under pressure and try to sell you things you don't want.

KEY:

1 f	3 a	5 e
2 d	4 b	6 c

3 Ask students to look at the example sentences to deduce the rules.

KEY:

1 a person/people = *who*
2 things = *that* or *which*
3 places = *where*

Language Practice

Follow the activity as directed in the Students' Book.

KEY:

1 A retailer is a person <u>who</u> sells to the customers in quantities <u>that</u> are convenient.
2 A retail outlet is the place <u>where</u> customers can purchase the goods
3 A supermarket is a store <u>which/that</u> sells a wide variety of goods.
4 A 'middleman' is a person <u>who</u> makes a profit by selling goods for more than s/he paid for them.
5 A speciality store is a retail outlet <u>which/that</u> sells a particular type of goods.

► **For more practice see Workbook page 24**

Writing

Read through the notes with the students to make sure they understand the material before writing. Point out that notes often do not use articles or relative clauses.

Business Communication

1 Telephoning. Show students that the diagram is divided into two parts – one part for speaking to a receptionist and the second part for when you are connected. You could select and follow a conversation through with phrases from the speech bubbles, or demonstrate with an able student. Students could then practise in pairs.

► **For more practice see Workbook page 26**

2 Through the switchboard. Ask students to predict what goes in the gaps then listen and check. Make sure students know that there are a number of possible answers.

KEY AND TAPESCRIPT 6.5 :

Conversation 1

(**R** = receptionist, **C** = caller)
R: Good morning, Dunton Associates.
C: Oh hello, ¹could I speak to Amanda Holt, please?
R: Just one moment. I'm afraid Ms Holt's line is busy.
C: ²Could you put me through to her secretary?
R: Just one moment. I'm afraid that line is busy, too. I can put you through to the message desk, if you like.
C: ³No thanks, I'll call back later.
R: Thank you. Goodbye.

Conversation 2

(**MG** = Melanie Grant, **BS** = Barry Smith)
R 2: Smith, Thomas and Manton.
MG: ⁴Could you put me through to Barry Smith, please?
R 2: It's ringing for you.
BS: Hello, Barry Smith speaking.
MG: ⁵Hello Mr Smith, it's Melanie Grant here.
BS: Hello, Ms Grant.

3 📼 6.6 Direct line. Look at the cartoon and ask students why it is a good idea to get a direct line.

KEY AND TAPESCRIPT 6.6:

Conversation 1

CP = Chris Parry, **PS** = Pat Summers, **JC** = Joanna Coutts

JC: Hello, Joanna Coutts. How may I help you?
CP: ¹Hello. This is Chris Parry. Could I speak to Pat Summers, please?
JC: I'm afraid she's out of the office at the moment. Can I get her to call you?
CP: ²Yes, please.
JC: Can you give me your number?
CP: ³03071 888935
JC: And, I'm sorry, your name again?
CP: ⁴Chris Parry.
JC: OK Ms Parry, I'll ask her to call you.
CP: Thank you.
JC: Thank you. Goodbye.
CP: Goodbye.

Conversation 2

PS: Hello, Pat Summers.
CP: ⁵Oh, hello Pat. It's Chris Parry here.
PS: Hello Chris. How are you?
CP: Fine thanks ...

Final Task

Make sure that Student A has got the information he/she needs from the Listening activity.

Checklist

3 advantage = convenience
disadvantage = security problems
4 Country of registration, manufacturer's/supplier's code, product and package size, price
5 Indefinite article = *a* or *an*
retail outlet is the only countable noun in the list

Troubleshooting, Company History and Retailing

1 Business Review

Direct the students to the text (have any of them heard of Selfridges?) and ask them to answer questions 1–6.

> Selfridges is a department store which began trading over 85 years ago. It is based in Oxford Street and is London's second largest department store after Harrods, with 150,000 m² of retail space. In the 1990s the store experienced some problems with its image because people thought the store was old-fashioned.
>
> To solve the problem, Selfridges invested £50m to re-establish the business as one of the capital's main shopping attractions. They decided to offer a wide choice of products to attract more customers. They built a huge central 'atrium' or entrance hall, and a series of new stores. Some of the stores are redesigned and others, such as Children's World, have their own restaurant.

These questions require students to review some of the issues discussed in units 4–6. Questions 1 and 2 focus on describing a company (Business Communication, unit 5). Questions 3 and 4 focus on troubleshooting strategies (unit 4) and questions 2 and 5 on retailing (unit 6).

1 Selfridges is 85 years old (began trading 85 years ago). It is a department store and is based in Oxford Street, in London. It has 500,000 square feet. of retail space (150,000m²).
2 Harrods is the store's main competitor.
3 The store had problems with its image – it was considered old-fashioned.
4 They invested £50m to re-design the store and now offer customers a wider choice of products.
5 A central atrium (glass dome) and restaurants in some of the stores.
6 experienced, invested, decided

2

- **IMG** had a problem with their image and had models on their books who were not bringing in any money. They appointed a new MD to raise the profile of the company and to increase profits.
- **Ford** realises that women make up 40% of the new car market. Many women are not happy with car manufacturers' products and services and consider the advertising to be aimed exclusively at men. In order to address these problems, Ford set up a 'spy team' to make sure that their products and services meet the needs of female customers.

- **Marks and Spencer** formed a partnership in 1894. In 1930 they opened their Marble Arch store in London. In 1975 M&S opened stores two Paris and Brussels and in 1988 they opened two stores in Hong Kong.
- **Bic** was founded in 1950. Between 1950 and 1953, Lazlo Biro invented the first pen, Marcel Bich refined and modified the design and Bich negotiated with Biro to produce and sell the pen. In 1953 production of the Bic "Crystal" began and in 1956, sales of the biro rose to a million a day. In 1972, Bic invented the disposable lighter and in 1975 they invented the throwaway razor. Nowadays they are also manufacturing windsurfing boards.
- **EMI** EMI first introduced LPs in 1948. These were followed in 1952 by 45 rpm vinyl singles and then in 1958 by the introduction of stereo LP records. Eight years later EMI introduced the first recording on cassette then, seventeen years after that in 1983, the company introduced its first compact discs. In 1994 EMI invested in VIVA, a music video channel. Today EMI is one of the world's leading music companies.
- **IKEA** is proud of its functional design, good quality materials and amazingly low prices; they call it 'Democratic Design'.

Vocabulary Review

Direct the students to the task, see how many of the following they can recall.

> 1 strategy: **c** plan
> 2 SWOT analysis: **f** an analysis of a company's situation
> 3 troubleshooting: **g** solving problems
> 4 established: **a** founded
> 5 founder: **e** the person who started the company
> 6 goods: **l** products
> 7 services: **b** industries where people do or provide something rather than produce something financial advice
> 8 retail outlet shop: **i** shop
> 9 profit margin: **j** the difference between how much it costs to produce goods and the price the consumer pays for them
> 10 supermarket: **k** a large self-service shop selling different brands of everyday goods
> 11 'remote' shopping: **h** shopping from home via the Internet or by TV shopping channel
> 12 mail order: **d** shopping from home by choosing goods from a company's catalogue

Grammar Review

Ask students to scan the advert and identify the job, and the qualities the candidate should have. Point out that there are four paragraphs and ask students to complete the tasks for paragraphs 1–3.

1

Sales Assistant

1 We are a large department store which [1]<u>began</u> trading in 1895. Our famous textiles department [2]<u>opened</u> in 1920 and quickly [3]<u>became</u> very popular.

2 We are looking for [4]Ø motivated Sales Assistants to work within [5]<u>a</u> variety of departments around [6]<u>the</u> store. These positions are available for [7]Ø one year.

3 The ideal candidate [8]<u>should</u> have at least 6 to 12 months' experience of working in a retail environment, and [9]<u>should</u> be familiar with department stores. These roles are very demanding and applicants [10]<u>should</u> be committed and hard-working.

4 If you are interested in the above positions, please call in to our Recruitment Centre for an application form.

---

2 and 3

1 **c** A management consultant is a person **who** gives advice to companies.
2 **e** Ford is a company **which/that** manufactures cars.
3 **a** Bic is a company **which/that** produces disposable products.
4 **b** A shopping centre is a place **where** customers can find many different shops.
5 **d** Barcodes are patterns of stripes **which/that** an electronic scanner reads.

Writing Review

Encourage students to make specific recommendations about how they will improve. It may be useful to draw up your own SWOT analysis of the group (not specific to any students) and discuss it with them.

Business Communication Review

Make sure students understand their roles and give them time to practise and to look up any phrases they need but have forgotten.
Walk around the classroom and listen as the students roleplay, then give feedback as a class.

Reading

Look at the business cards. For questions 1–6 below decide which of the business cards A–H could be helpful to each of the people listed.

Use each card only once.

A

Chen Lee
Computer Consultant
Lee Communications Ltd.

B

Yosuhiro Ito

Advertising Executive
CR & THG Media Ltd

C

Susanne Gaueret

MANAGER

GAUERET EUROPEAN FREIGHT CO.

D

Esme Klein
Customer Services
London Bank

E

E. Maria Castillon
Personnel Manager
European Business Press

F

William Mills
Telecommunications Engineer
English Telecom

G

Pauline Yin

TRAVEL CO-ORDINATOR

ANGLO-CHINA TRAVEL SERVICES

H

Martin Boyle
Managing Director
Mackem Retail Group

1 Ms Kim wants to get a job in publishing.
2 Mr Stamp's boss has told him to get information about new computer systems for the firm's office.
3 Mrs Bacon needs to send her company's products to Hungary.
4 Mr Lange is responsible for the launch of new products for his company.
5 Ms Singh's company is looking for a bank loan.
6 Mrs O'Neill needs to arrange a visit to China for her company's sales director.

Speaking

Candidate A

You need to ask Candidate B for information about a company.

Your Questions

Company Name:	_____	Products:	_____
Location of head office:	_____	Profits last year:	_____
Number of employees:	_____		

Your Information

Name:	European Business Press	**Business:**	Publishers of books about business
Head office:	London	**Founded:**	1972
Parent company:	International Press Ltd.		
Profits last year:	£750,000 (3 quarters of a million)	**Profits previous year:**	£1,834,000
Offices:	London, Paris, Rome	**Employees:**	315
Plans:	re-structure the business		

✂ •

Speaking

Candidate B

You need to ask Candidate A for information about a company.

Your Questions

Company Name:	_____	Industry/area of business:	_____
Founded:	_____	Location of head office:	_____
Plans:	_____		

Your Information

Name:	Fizz Co.	**Business:**	Manufacturers of soft drinks
Head office:	Manchester	**Founded:**	1969
Owners:	Big Foods Ltd.	**Profits last year:**	£16,360, 000 (£16.3 million)
		Profits previous year:	£13,300, 000 (£13.3 million)
Offices:	Manchester, New York	**Employees:**	7,250
Plans:	Expand in East Europe		

Writing

You are going on a computer training course on Friday from 10.00 a.m.–3.00 p.m.

Write a memo to your boss, Marcia Auger, to remind her:

- of the date and time of the course
- that you can't come to the lunch-time meeting
- you will be back in the office at 3.30 p.m.

Write about 20–30 words.

MEMO

To:

From:

Date:

Subject:

• •

Listening

For questions 1 and 2 you will hear two short recordings.
For each question, mark A, B or C for the most suitable answer.

Question 1

How much are the tickets that the woman buys?

a £10

b £20

c £150

Question 2

Which business is the company going to sell?

a cinema

b theatre

c sports centre

Question 3

• **Look at the notes below.**

• **You will hear a manager discussing a visit by the Health and Safety inspectors with his secretary.**

• **Listen to the conversation and write in the missing numbers.**

• **You will hear the conversation twice.**

Health and safety inspectors visit on (1) _____ October

2 inspectors arrive at (2) _____

Interview with (3) _____ Production Supervisors

Coffee at (4) _____

Products

Further information about a company discussed in this unit can be found at this website:

> Dyson: http://www.dyson.com

If your students have access to the Internet, you could ask them to do research from the company website.

Key Vocabulary

🔲 **7.1** Read through the Key Vocabulary text with the students. Make sure that they can pronounce as well as use the words by playing the recorded version.

You may like to use the cloze version of the Key Vocabulary. (► page 95). You could give it to your students to see how many of the words phrases they know before beginning the unit.

► **For more practice see Workbook page 30**

Lead-in

1 Direct students look at all four photos on the page then listen to the tape.

TAPESCRIPT 7.2:

Salesperson: We are proud to present this important new addition to our range. It comes with active speakers and its great new colours are stylish and fashionable. As well as the speakers, we offer you all the features you normally expect – this high-spec product has a 22-track programmable memory, random play and more. We think you'll find £79.99 is an amazing price, and we're sure you'll be keen to order your personal player right away.

KEY: CD player

2 To demonstrate the task, discuss each of the questions for the File Organiser as a class.

KEY:

Features:
2000 File Organiser: small electronic organiser, can be used with your computer.
Solar watch: smart watch powered by solar energy.
Aerobic workout machine: exercise machine for men and women.
CD player: small, fashionably coloured compact disc player.

Benefits/USP:
2000 file organiser: PC data link/low price .
Solar watch: doesn't need batteries.
Aerobic workout machine: workout in the comfort of your home.

CD player: a flexible high-specification product with a competitive price.

Language Focus One

1 Direct the students to the picture and then ask them to complete labelling 1–4.

KEY:

1 handle	3 trim
2 shoulder strap	4 lock

2 Find out which briefcases students prefer and why. Then ask them to match the descriptions with the pictures.

KEY:

1 c	2 a	3 e	4 b	5 d

3 Check that students understand the difference between opinion and fact.

KEY: - see table below

4 and **5**

	OPINION	FACT					
		size/length	shape/width	colour	where it's from	what it's made of	
①	stylish					leather	briefcase
	beautiful					glass	handle
②							briefcase
	practical					nylon	straps
				black			trim
③				black	Italian		briefcase
		long					strap
④	elegant				light brown	leather	briefcase
						brass	locks
⑤	durable					leather	briefcase
						brass	locks

	size/length	shape/width	colour	where it's from	what it's made of	
	big	square			leather	folder
	large	extra wide				sports bag
	spacious	oval				handbag

6 KEY:
1 before 'fact' adjectives
2 size, shape, age, colour, origin, material, type
3 Size goes before shape.

Language Practice One

1 Elicit which of the adjectives students could use to describe the filofax from the box (*smart, useful, expensive*) then ask them what other adjectives they could use to describe it, ask (*What colour is it? What's it made of?*).

▶ **For more practice see Workbook page 31**

Reading

1 Questions 1 and 2 are to be done before reading.

2 Check students understand the different adjectives in the box and elicit which ones they think describe the vacuum cleaners. Ask them to say why.

4 Students scan the extract quickly.

KEY:

a 1978 – Dyson had the idea for the vacuum cleaner.
b 5 – years before a working model was completed.
c 5,127 – The number of prototypes that he made.
d 23 – The number of months after the launch that the Dyson became Britain's best-selling vacuum cleaner.

5 KEY:

1 15 years. This is unusual.
2 Because he developed something completely new. He didn't have any model to work from.
3 Hoover, Electrolux, Panasonic, Miele
4 His business is extremely successful, producing the market leader in vacuum cleaners.

6 Ask students to read the article and answer exercises 6 and 7.

KEY:

1 He won the European Design Prize.
2 It doesn't have a bag to collect the dust.
3 He got backing from the US and Japan. The British seem not to be aware of the importance of innovation.

7 Close and careful reading is required.

KEY:

1 = b   2 = c   3 = d   4 = e   5 = a

Vocabulary

1 Check that students can pronounce the words.

KEY:

to get 'backing   to in'vent a ma'chine
to steal an i'dea   to win a 'prize

2 KEY:

1 won a prize   3 steal idea
2 invented a machine   4 get backing

3 KEY:

1 award   2 to invent   3 inventor   4 to develop
5 developer   6 innovation   7 competitor

4

1 innovative/innovators   3 develop
2 invention   4 award competition

Writing

1 Read through the examples with the students and check they understand the difference between cause and effect. Draw students' attention to the positioning of the words/phrases.

2 Read through the examples with the students and check they understand all the vocabulary.

KEY:

The following are suggestions.
1 **Because** the cost of raw materials increased, the price of manufactured goods increased too.
2 All the manufacturers refused to back the design **so** the inventor produced the new vacuum cleaner himself.
3 **Since** the product is not selling well, we need to review our marketing strategy.
4 The company set the price of the product too high and **as a result**, demand was low.

▶ **For more practice see Workbook page 34**

Language Focus Two

KEY

1, 2 and 3

a -er   b less or more   c than

a the -est   b the most   the least

as + adjective + *as*

Pronunciation

1 🔲 7.3 Play the tape and elicit how the endings are pronounced.

2 🔲 7.4 Stop and repeat after each phrase.

3 🔲 7.5 Play the tape through once and elicit how *than* and *as* are pronounced. Play the tape again, pausing after each sentence for students to repeat.

4 Make sure students use normal sentence stress.

Language Practice Two

2 Ask students to test each other by giving their partner two or three brands to compare in as many different ways they can in a set amount of time.

▶ **For more practice see Workbook page 31**

Listening

1 To check that students understand the two terms, ask them to discuss the questions in pairs.

KEY:

1 fmcgs 2 consumer durables 3 consumer durables

2 Check answers as a class.

KEY:

fmcgs:	Consumer durables:
clothes (both)	clothes (both)
beer	cars
canned drinks	computers
chocolate	CD player
wine (both)	wine (both)
fruit	televisions
meat	washing machines
envelopes	compact discs
	shoes

3 Follow the directions in the Students' Book. Alternatively, ask students to think of two fmcgs and two consumer durables and discuss with a partner how they are advertised.

4 🔲 **7.6** Encourage students to read through the questions before they listen to the tape.

TAPESCRIPT 7.6:

(**Int** = Interviewer, **VA** = Verena Adams)

Int: Verena, how important is advertising in selling products?

VA: Well, it's an important marketing tool, and it works in a number of different ways.

Int: What *are* some of the ways it can work?

VA: Advertising can inform or persuade or remind or motivate; obviously the type of ad depends on the product.

Int: Oh, I see, but could you give us an example?

VA: Well, erm, for example – a low cost, erm low cost fast moving consumer goods, erm like chocolate bars or soft drinks, erm are going to be advertised differently from consumer durables like televisions or washing machines. You'd advertise Tango differently from the way you'd advertise a car.

Int: Right, so how would a Tango advertisement work?

VA: Well, Tango's a fizzy drink, an orange fizzy drink in

a can, erm, so it's aimed at the teenage market. You'd go for eye-catching, attention-getting advertising; you'd try to create a modern brand image.

Int: Uh, huh.

VA: Erm, television ads which were created, erm, had a very crazy, funny, colourful campaign, erm aimed to motivate the teenage market to buy; and they were very successful.

Int: I see. How about advertising a car?

VA: Well for a car you're into a different product sector, erm, and a different target audience. You're trying to persuade that market to spend a lot of money, so you'd go for press ads, with lots of copy – details of the models and the prices and the features and all that kind of thing – and you'd probably back it up with a television campaign to show the cars in action.

Int: Who decides, then, who actually decides which sort of media to use?

VA: Erm, well, advertisers go for different mixes of media, erm but basically it's the advertising agency who makes the choices; the agency is the link between the manufacturer of the product and the public, and erm, they create a brief of the different, of the most suc... most useful kinds of media to use.

Int: What do you think makes a good advertisement, then?

VA: In my opinion, a good advertisement always concentrates on the product.

Play the tape again and stop it after the answer to each question. Go through the answers and check students understand the different ways that advertising can work (*inform, persuade, remind, motivate*).

KEY:

1 a marketing tool
2 It can inform, persuade, remind or motivate.

3	Tango	Car
Target audience:	teenage market	
Design of ad:	attention-getting to create a modern brand image	models, prices and features
Style of campaign:	funny and colourful	not given
Media:		a TV campaign
Purpose of ad:		persuade the market to spend a lot of money

4 The advertising agency is the link between the manufacturer and the public.
5 A good advertisement concentrates on the product.

▶ **For more practice see Workbook page 30**

Business Communication

1 📼 **7.7** Direct students to the picture of the Videophone in the picture. Find out if any of the students have used one. Check they understand the following expressions: *a touch-tone phone, software, on-screen*.

TAPESCRIPT 7.7:

Presenter: Do you have friends and family you would like to see more often? When you phone colleagues would you like to see their faces? The ViaTV Desktop Videophone means that you can!

As you can see it's small and elegant and ideal for the office or for the home or for business trips.

It's very easy to set up. All you need is a touch-tone phone. You don't need a computer and you don't need any special software. It's also very easy to use; it's as easy as making a normal telephone call. The ViaTV Desktop Videophone has many features. Firstly, it has full colour motion video which means you can see the other person's gestures and changes of expression.

The picture quality is excellent and the adjustable picture setting means you can change to 'sharp' mode to get a fantastically clear image. This, of course, is just ideal for viewing designs or documents. The audio quality is exactly the same as a normal telephone call.

In addition, the Via Desktop Videophone also has a preview mode so that you can check what you look like before the other person sees you! And finally, the privacy mode is an important feature. You can use it to block the image but keep voice connection.

Now, of course, just as with any means of communication, fax machines or e-mail for example, each party needs to have a set. We have a special offer on at the moment, so now is the time to buy the ViaTV Desktop phone. Put yourself in the picture.

KEY:

1 b 2 c 3 a 4 b 5 c

2 Play the tape again for students to answer.

KEY:

The main benefit is that you can see your caller's face (gestures and change of expression).
The target customer is probably a person who has family they would like to see more often or a business person doing business with overseas colleagues.

3 Students complete the summary using their answers to 1 and 2.

KEY:

1 ViaTV Desktop Videophone
2 small and elegant
3 a touch-tone phone
4 full colour motion video and very good picture quality.
5 a preview mode and a privacy mode
6 you can see your caller's face

4 Divide students into two groups and ask them to complete the summaries.

KEY:

Multi-lingual European Interpreter

Benefits: **You will never be lost for words.**
Your business trips will be easier and more enjoyable
Special features: • **7** languages
• **30,000** words per language
• **spelling correction**
• 30-entry **name/address databank**
• **calculator**
• **metric and currency converters**
Price: **£49.95**

Memo Recording Pen
Appearance: Stylish and compact
Benefits: You can easily record your ideas, thoughts, messages and reminders.
Special features: 2 ballpoint pen
• crisp, clear sound
• instant playback
Price: Free

5 For feedback, find out if the students managed to convince their partner to buy the product, if so how, if not why not.

Final Task

Ensure that students can justify their choice of product and describe its features.

Checklist

KEY:

1 smart, slim, blue, leather briefcase
2 reliable – more reliable, most reliable
  expensive – more expensive, most expensive
  soft – softer, softest
  light – lighter, lightest
  new – newer, newest
  stylish – more stylish, most stylish
3, 4 and 5 Ensure that students can justify their choice of answers

People

Key Vocabulary

📼 **8.1** Read through the Key Vocabulary text with the students. Make sure that they can pronounce as well as use the words by playing the recorded version. As a lead-in to the topic, ask students to brainstorm all the reasons they can think of why people work. Discuss as a class.

You may like to use the cloze version of the Key Vocabulary text. (▶ page 94). You could give it to your students to see how many of the words they know before beginning the unit.

▶ **For more practice see Workbook page 35**

Lead-in

1 Direct students to the different factors listed in the Students' Book. Be prepared to explain any items they do not understand. Encourage students to compare the factors they consider most important with their partner and to explain why.

Cross-cultural Communication

In a multinational class, try and organise students into groups with as many different nationalities as possible. In a monolingual class, encourage students to compare their own country with another which they know well. Check that students understand *counsellor*. Find out which of the three roles students consider to be the most important.

Language Focus One

Before playing the tape make sure that the students know that an *appraisal* is a regular meeting (usually every six months) between the employee and his/her line manager at which performance is discussed and goals defined.

1 📼 **8.2** If the students are already working, find out if they have regular appraisals, and if so, what their purpose is.

TAPESCRIPT 8.2:

(**PT** = Philippa Taylor, **DG** = Dan Goldman)

PT: Right, Dan. You know that the aim of this performance appraisal is to look at how you're doing and to identify any areas where you need to make some changes.
So, what's your assessment? How are you getting on?

DG: Pretty good, I guess. I'm really enjoying the work here.

PT: That's good to hear. Is there anything you're particularly pleased with?

DG: Erm, yeah. I was very pleased with the way things went on the Silverton project. It was a great team – really motivating to work with them, and to learn from them.

PT: Good, yes, I think you worked really well on that project....

PT: OK. So now are there any aspects of the job where you think there is room for improvement?

DG: Well, I'm still having some difficulties with my time management.

PT: Why do you think that is?

DG: I guess I'm a bit too optimistic about how much I can do in a day! But I really do want to get better at organising my time.

PT: OK. So what are you going to do about that?

DG: Well, I'm going to try to prioritise more, to deal with the things that are really important. I'm also going to set myself more realistic deadlines.

PT: Good, OK, that sounds sensible.

DG: And, I've finally got a place on a time management course and I'm doing that next month.

PT: Excellent. Who's running it this time?

DG: It's Scott Henman.

PT: Oh, he's good. I think that will be very useful.

KEY:

He is (really) ¹<u>enjoying the work</u>.
He is particularly pleased with ²<u>the Silverton project</u>.

He's going to ³<u>try to prioritise more</u>
He's going to ⁴<u>set himself realistic deadlines</u>.
Scott Henman ⁵<u>is running</u> the course.

2 and 3

KEY:

2a future plans and intentions = *going to*
  b definite future arrangements = present continuous for future
3 True

Pronunciation One

1 📼 **8.2b** Play the tape and elicit the pronunciation of *to*.

2 📼 **8.3** Play the tape, pausing after each question for students to repeat.
NOTE With *wh-* questions there is usually a falling intonation at the end of the question.

3 Listen to the students as they are asking and answering the questions and check that they are using the correct stress and intonation.

Language Practice One

1 Ask students to work in pairs and match the people with the action points.

KEY:

Aleka: 1, 4, 9   Juan: 2, 3, 5   Chan: 6, 7, 8

2 Point out that these are things that Juan, Aleka and Chan have already thought about and plan to do. Elicit from students which tense to use (*going to*).

KEY:

(Suggested answers)
Aleka is going to find out more about computers to find the right one for her.
Juan is going to talk to a careers consultant.
Chan is going to leave work earlier.

3 Encourage students to think about both short-term and long-term objectives and to write down an action plan for each. They discuss this with their partner. Encourage students to give their partners further advice using *should/ought to*.

▶ **For more practice see Workbook page 36**

Language Focus Two

NOTE The Inland Revenue is the department of the UK government that raises/collects taxes inside the UK.

1 Focus attention on the advertisement and the first four general comprehension questions.

KEY:

1 The Inland Revenue
2 Graduates
3 Fast Stream Development Programme
4 'Free thinking' i.e. creative people

2 KEY:

1 give	3 learn/see	5 discriminate
2 give	4 need	6 will not

Pronunciation Two

1 🔲 **8.4** Play the tape once and elicit how *will/will not* are pronounced. Play the tape again pausing after each sentence for students to repeat.

2 KEY:

a True   b True   c True   d False   e True

Language Practice Two

1 Follow the activity as directed in the Students' Book. Ask students to write the full sentences and then practise saying them in pairs.

KEY:

(Suggested answers)
1 You will learn about management.
2 We will offer you excellent training.
3 You will earn between £14,000 and £21,000 a year.
4 You will need to take some exams.
5 The Inland Revenue will not discriminate against you.
6 You will be expected to live in Southern England.

2 Monitor and check that they are pronouncing the short form of *will* correctly.

▶ **For more practice see Workbook page 37**

3 Divide students into pairs and ask them to follow the activity as directed in the Students' Book.

Listening

1 🔲 **8.5** Explain that students are going to hear someone describing various aspects of work. Before you play the tape, ask students to read through the notes and check that they understand the expression *to get on with it*. Tell the students that you are going to play the tape through once without any stops and that they should note down any information which they think is important. Play the tape again, pausing to give students time to complete their notes.

TAPESCRIPT 8.5:

(**Int** = Interviewer, **ML** = Morna Lawson)

Int: Can you tell me what gives you satisfaction in your job?

ML: Well, there's different things really, er, obviously salary is important, status is important – I want to be respected for what I do – erm, but most importantly I can't bear being bored, with routines, so I want the freedom to develop my role, really.

Int: So it's important your manager gives you autonomy?

ML: Yes.

Int: What management style do you respond well to?

ML: Well, I like them, really I like my manager to be fairly hands-off, yet available, so I'm allowed to do what, I'm allowed to get on with it and the manager is there to support me.

Int: OK. I know you've worked in Spain and Britain. Are there any differences between the workplace culture in the two countries?

ML: Mmm, it was a while, a few years ago that I was in Spain, and I think that Britain and Spain have probably become more similar, but the thing I noticed most was that the Spanish work in order to enjoy their lives far more so than they do in Britain.

Int: Right, could you describe your best manager?

ML: Erm, a woman I worked with in Spain, who enjoyed her job, enjoyed life; we had a good time at work, erm, and most of all she allowed me to get on with it, make my mistakes – it wasn't the end of the world, and I learnt a lot from it.

KEY:

1 **Job satisfaction**
   salary   status   freedom to develop her role
2 **Management styles**
   ᵃhands-off   ᵇavailable.   ᶜsupport
3 **Workplace culture**
   the Spanish work in order to enjoy their lives more than the British do.
4 **Managers**
   ᵃa woman she worked with in Spain.
   ᵇmake mistakes   ᶜlearnt a lot from it.

2 Check that students understand the vocabulary in the list. Ask students to compare their answers in pairs and to discuss the other points that Morna made.

3 Ask students to choose the phrases that match what Morna said. Students discuss in small groups or as a class the workplace culture in their own country. You could also ask them to compare it with other countries they know.

Reading

NOTE The focus of the unit is on management styles, not on gender. You may want to make the tone of this text quite light.

1 As a lead-in, find out if students think that men and women have different working styles. Focus attention on the cartoons and ask students to discuss in pairs which figures they think represent men and which represent women. Check that students understand the captions.

2 Students read the text to see if the writer agrees which cartoons are predominantly male and which are predominantly female.

3 Students read the text again and match the cartoons to each subheading.

KEY:

   male = a b d e   female = c f g h i

4 This exercise requires fairly careful reading of the text. It is probably worth going through the first few phrases as a class to demonstrate the task. Ask students to underline the section in the text which confirms their ideas.

KEY:

1 But we need to take account of ... = women because 'the female preference is to look at various options.' (para 2)
2 Women because 'women tend to welcome others opinions.' (para 4)
3 Men because 'the male approach to business is competitive, direct and confrontational.' (para 1)
4 Men because they 'find it easy to tell others about their successes.' (para 7)
5 Women because they 'tend to share or pass on the credit for a success.' (para 7)
6 Men because 'a man's joke usually has a victim.' (para 8)

5 Discuss as a class.

6 Divide students into groups of between four and six. (Depending on the composition of your class, you may want to mix the sexes up or ask students to discuss this in male groups and female groups to see if their opinions differ.) If possible, encourage students to draw on their own work experience here.

Vocabulary

1 and **2** Ask students to refer back to the text to find words to complete the table. Highlight the stress on *com'pete, compe'tition* and *com'petitive*. Students then complete the sentences in 2. Encourage students to check the word stress in a dictionary.

KEY:

confron'tational   col'laborative
con'trol   to en'courage
a'chievement

2 KEY

1 achievement   4 collaborate
2 encouragement   5 control
3 confrontational

Writing

1 Read through the sample sentences with the students. Draw students' attention to the positioning of the conjunctions and that make sure they introduce the clause of contrast.

2 Direct students' attention to the chart of CEOs' pay. You may like to provide a sample or two of what the exercise requires. Check that students understand *basic pay*, *bonus* and *perks*. Highlight the examples that are given in the Students' Book and ask students to try and rewrite them using *but* and *however*.

▶ **For more practice see Workbook page 38**

Business Communication

1 Find out if any of the students know any tour representatives. If so, ask them to describe what the job involves or ask students to imagine what the job involves.

2 8.6 Tell students that they are going to hear a tour representative describing her job. Remind students what 'perks' are. Ask them to read through the notes and play the tape for them to complete the notes. Find out if they are surprised by any of the things she mentions. Why do they think that there are more women than men in her company?

TAPESCRIPT 8.6:

Int = Interviewer, LC= Lisa Crawford

Int: What do you do?
LC: I work in the travel industry. I'm a tour representative for Sun Travel.
Int: That sounds fun. What does the job involve?
LC: Well it's not all sun and sea. In fact it's often very hard work. Basically, it involves looking after people when they're on holiday. I'm responsible for sorting out any problems and I often have to deal with complaints. The work also involves entertaining the holidaymakers and their children.
Int: It sounds like hard work. But what about the perks?
LC: Well, the obvious one is that you get to travel a lot and experience different cultures. I really value that aspect of the work.
Int: What about your colleagues? Are they mainly men or women?
LC: In the company I work for there are more women than men, but I'm not sure that that's true of the industry as a whole.

KEY:

Name:	Lisa Crawford
Job Title:	Tour Representative
Company she works for:	Sun Travel
Perks:	lots of travel and experience of different cultures
Ratio men:women	more women than men

3 Play the tape again and draw students' attention to the language pattern box in the Students' Book. Draw students' attention to the verb patterns.

KEY:

1 It involves *looking after people when they're on holiday.*
2 I'm responsible for *sorting out any problems.*
3 I have to deal with *complaints.*
4 It also involves *entertaining the holidaymakers.*

4 8.7 Play the tape once and elicit which job the speaker describes. Ask students which expressions they heard which told them this.

KEY:

Personnel Officer

5 Divide the students into pairs. Monitor and check that students are using the verb patterns correctly.

6 Give students time to make notes about their job and help them with any difficult language.

7 Divide the students into pairs for this exercise.

Final Task

Give students some suggestions about how to lay this out, e.g.

Objectives: (1) To get a new job
Action plan: I'm going to re-write my CV.

Checklist

1 *going to*
2 when talking generally about the future
3 *won't*
4 achievement

unit 9

Business Environment

Further information about the companies mentioned in this unit is available at these websites:

> IKEA: http://www.ikea.com
> Rover: http://www.rovercars.com
> Nissan: http://nissan-europe.com
> Vauxhall: http://vauxhall.co.uk
> Peugeot: http://peugeot.com
> Marks and Spencer: http://www.marks-and-spencer.com

If your students have access to the Internet, you could ask them to do research from the company websites.

Key Vocabulary

9.1 As a lead-in to the subject, tell students that a foreign company wishes to open a new dairy producing yogurts, cheeses, etc. in your country for export to EU countries. Divide students into small groups to discuss: *Where should the dairy be located? Why?*

Read through the Key Vocabulary text with the students. Make sure that the students can pronounce as well as use the words by playing the recorded version. It might help to ask them how the variables mentioned here, such as availability of labour, have affected a local industry, if relevant.

You may like to use the cloze version of the Key Vocabulary text. (➤ page 96). You could give it to your students to see how many of the words they know before beginning the unit.

➤ **For more practice see Workbook page 40**

Lead-in

Focus attention on the shopping baskets and then ask the students to discuss the five questions.
They can then check their answers to question 5 by reading the text in exercise 2.

KEY:

1 Japan   2 US   3 $42
4 Everyday groceries
5 Differences in exchange rates, differences in local raw materials, labour costs, import and other taxes, – see text in Exercise 2.

Language Focus One

1 Check that students know what a Big Mac is (a type of hamburger from McDonald's). Focus attention on 'The Big Mac Index' and on the information for Lagos, then look at the opening example. Students

complete question 1 in pairs. Discuss 2 as a class.

KEY:

Nairobi 177 minutes   Caracas   243 minutes
London   38 minutes   Budapest 128 minutes

2 **9.2** Play the tape while students read through the questions. Find out if the students think the woman is sure about what she is saying or making guesses.

KEY:

She is guessing. Hence: 'may be, might, could, I could be wrong but I think, it can't be, perhaps, probably'.

3 You may want to use this exercise for a class discussion.

KEY:

1 True   2 True

Pronunciation One

1 **9.3a** Play the tape once for students to answer the question. Play the tape again and ask students to repeat each word.

2 **9.3b** Play the tape for students to answer the question.

3 Elicit which 'following words' start with vowels and which start with consonants. Write the following rules on the board:

– When the following word starts with a consonant, the final letter ..... pronounced. (*isn't*)

– When the following word starts with a vowel, the final letter ..... pronounced. (*is*)

Ask students to complete the rules.

4 Play the tape again, pausing the tape after each sentence for students to repeat.

Language Practice One

1 Ask students to look at the 'facts' column and then match them with possible reasons. What other possible reasons can students think of?

KEY:

1 d   2 b   3 c   4 a

2 **9.4** Remind students that they have already looked at IKEA. (Unit 6) Find out what they can remember about it. Focus attention on the two pie charts. Point out that the first is for sales and the second is for purchases. Tell students to fill in the names of the countries and parts of the world as they listen to the tape.

62

TAPESCRIPT 9.4 and KEY:

BA = Business Analyst

BA: OK, let's start with some news about IKEA. The Swedish furniture giant has continued to do excellent business this year. IKEA has a global presence with stores in around 30 countries and it is continuing to expand, opening new stores every year. Its biggest market is Europe with sales accounting for 84.4% of total sales. Within Europe, Scandinavia, Germany, France and the UK are very significant markets. Of these, Germany is the largest, with France, Scandinavia and the UK having almost equal shares.

North [1]America accounts for 14.4 % of sales and [2]Asia for 1.2%.

IKEA's products are designed and developed in Sweden by IKEA Sweden, but manufactured all over the world. IKEA has suppliers in 65 countries. 19.2% of the suppliers are in the [3]Far East and 17.2% in [4]East Central Europe. Just 3.3% are in [5]North America. IKEA's success depends on these local suppliers, so before opening a store in a new market, IKEA establishes a link with a supplier in that market. It chooses carefully; criteria for selecting suppliers may include proximity to raw materials, reliable access to distribution channels and low costs ...

3 Look at the example as a class then students discuss the reasons in pairs. Monitor and check that they are using the target language correctly.

► **For more practice see Workbook page 42**

Cross-cultural Comparison

Before students discuss the chart, it may be necessary to check that they understand *political stability* and *infrastructure*. Encourage as much speculation as you can about these figures.

Listening

🔲 9.5 **1** and **2** Before you play the tape, you might want to check that students understand *economic restructuring* and *reunification*. Suggest that the first time students listen, they complete the country and position and then play the tape again for them to fill in the reason. Find out if any of the students guessed the reasons correctly.

TAPESCRIPT 9.5:

(**TA** = Tom Armstrong)

TA: I'm going to talk about the world's most competitive countries, and to do this we are using an index, where we can see that the United States of America is at the top of the index, and the questions we must ask are 'why are some countries higher than others?'

America is at the top of the index because of continuous economic growth. We note that the Netherlands is Europe's highest competitor, or best competitor, in fourth position, and this again is because of a successful economic restructuring.

Singapore comes in the second position, at number two – it is the most technologically advanced economy in the world.

Perhaps surprisingly Germany is below countries such as Canada and Britain, and is in 14th place, as a result of a reunification process which is very, very expensive.

Brazil is equivalent to Greece and the Czech Republic in having problems with infrastructure, and finds itself in 37th position.

KEY:

COUNTRY	POSITION	REASON
1 United States	Top/1st	continuous economic growth
2 Netherlands	4th (top European country)	successful economic restructuring
3 Singapore	2nd	technologically advanced economy
4 Germany	14th	re-unification process is very expensive
5 Brazil	37th	problems with infrastructure (like Greece and the Czech Republic)

Writing

1 and **2** Read through the examples with the students and discuss how they are used.

KEY:

1 a **too, as well** (they are interchangeable) usually come at the end of a clause or sentence.
2 c **in addition** can be used to begin a second sentence which adds additional information to the first sentence, but usually begins a second clause, often following 'and ...'
3 b **also** usually comes in the middle of the sentence, linking two pieces of information

3
KEY:

1 in addition
2 also
3 in addition
4 in addition
5 also
6 too/as well

➤ **For more practice see Workbook page 43**

Language Focus Two

1 and **2** Students look at the graphic, discuss the car manufacturers and write the nationalities on the graphic. Check that they pronounce the nationalities correctly. Ask students to complete the sentences and check their answers in pairs.

KEY:

1 The Vauxhall Sintra is made in Dorrevill, USA.
2 The Nissan Primera is built in Sunderland, UK.
3 The Fiat Seicento is made in Tychy, Poland.
4 The Rover 200 is built in Oxford and Birmingham, UK.
5 The Peugeot 206 is built in Ryton, UK, and more than 50% of parts are sourced in the UK. The rest come from other EC countries.

3 Discuss the questions as a class.

KEY:

1 No
2 No, it is *not* clear who carries out the action in each sentence.
3 It is not important to know who carries out the action. We are interested in the action not the 'doer'.

4 Follow the activity as directed in the Students' Book.

KEY:

1 We form a passive with the correct part of the verb *to be* + the past *participle*.
2 The *object* of an active verb becomes the *subject* of a passive verb.
3 In *passive* sentences you do not need to include the 'doer', i.e. the person or thing which performs the action, because this is not an important piece of information.

Language Practice Two

1 Follow the activity as directed in the Students' Book.

KEY:

The engines ¹*are manufactured* at Ellesmere Port in the UK. The cars ²*are built* in the US and ³*are sold* there as the Pontiac. Cars ⁴*are shipped* back to the UK and ⁵*are sold* as the Sintra.

2 Find out if students know how interactive telephone services work and whether they have used them. As the vocabulary in this exercise is quite tricky, go through the diagram with the students and check that they understand what is happening at each stage. Then students complete the sentences.

3 **KEY:**

1 A telephone enquiry *is made*.
2 The speech *is changed* to digital code.
3 The digitised sounds *are compared* with those on the computer and *are analysed* for meaning.
4 The appropriate information *is collected* from the computer database.
5 The information *is converted* to text.
6 The text *is converted* to speech.

4 Some suggestions are as follows:
paying for something by credit card
finding out a share price over the Internet
checking emails
programming the video player

➤ **For more practice see Workbook page 42**

Reading

1–7 Remind students that they have already looked at Marks and Spencer earlier in the course. What can they remember about it?

KEY:

1 Profits were poor at the time of writing.
2 Retailing and financial services. The financial services are doing well. .
3 Home furnishings, food, clothing and footwear are all mentioned. M&S are about to expand their food operations.
4 The Far East, Europe and North America.
5 Down in all three markets.
6 and 7
1 Far East – **c** suffered a downturn (economic turmoil)
2 Europe – **a** profits were hit (the strong pound)
3 North America – **b** profits fell (no explanation given)

Vocabulary

The language of describing rises and falls is, obviously, important in business.

1 and **2** Ask the students to complete the table.

KEY:

VERBS	NOUNS
to improve	an improvement
to rise	a rise
to increase	an increase
to grow	

VERBS	NOUNS
to maintain	
to stabilise	

VERBS	NOUNS
to fall	a fall
to decline	a decline
to decrease	a decrease
to drop	a drop

Pronunciation Two

1 🔲 **9.6a** Play the tape with pauses for students to repeat the words and practise the stressing of nouns and verbs.

2 🔲 **9.6b** Play the tape and ask students to write down if they hear the noun or verb. Ask students to practise this in pairs. One student could read out four words and his/her partner write down whether they hear the noun or the verb, then they change roles.

TAPESCRIPT 9.6B and KEY:

1. We <u>increase</u> sales every year. (verb)
2. We need <u>an increase</u> in sales. (noun)
3. We want <u>to decrease</u> the costs. (verb)
4. They won't accept <u>a decrease</u> in their salaries. (noun)
5. <u>Exports</u> cost too much. (noun)
6. We hope <u>to increase</u> <u>exports</u>. (verb) (noun)
7. We need <u>to decrease</u> <u>imports</u>. (verb) (noun)

Business Communication

Describing trends
Follow the activity as directed in the Students' Book.

1 KEY:
1. *From* 1993 *to* 1994 registrations rose *by* about 7,000.
2. There was a decrease *of* about 2.3 million from 1992 to 1993.
3. Car registrations rose *from* about 11.2 million in 1993 *to* about 12.8 million in 1996.

2 KEY
1. biggest decrease – 1992–1993
2. biggest increase – 1995–1996
3. smallest increase – 1994–1995
4. smallest decrease – 1997–1998

3

TAPESCRIPT 9.7:

1. Sales increased slightly from 1991 to 1992.
2. Sales decreased dramatically from 1992 to 1993.
3. In 1993 sales improved significantly.
4. Sales rose from 1993 to 1994.
5. Sales grew steadily from 1994 to 1997.
6. Sales fell sharply from 1999 to 2000.

KEY:

1 F	3 T	5 T
2 T	4 T	6 T

Final Task

1 Divide the class into Students A and B. Student A describes cinema attendances in Poland, Germany and Britain to student B, and Student B describes those of France and Italy. Together they complete the graph.

2 Elicit possible reasons for the trend and make sure that students remember to use expressions for possibility correctly.

3 Remind students of the connectors they studied in the unit.

Checklist

1. labour costs, costs of raw materials, differing taxes, etc.
2. *may, might, could, can*
3. When the 'doer' is not important and we wish to emphasise what would be the object of an active sentence.
4. *to decrease, to drop, to fall, to decline*, etc.
5. *to increase, to rise, to grow, to climb*, etc.

Products, People and the Business Environment

Business Review

Direct the students to the short text and ask them to answer questions 1–4.

> The Internet offers a real opportunity for retailers and service providers to advertise their goods and services. Banking is a growth area, and many banks now offer Internet banking services. Most Net users are married males in their 30s. Security is the number one concern for users, and they are asked to register a security pass code each time they access their account.

Questions 1 and 2 review product descriptions (Unit 7). Question 3 reviews the Business Environment topic and question 4 reviews the use of the passive voice (Unit 9).

1 'Remote' or Internet banking is becoming popular. It is easy to access 24 hours per day. You can access your bank account from your own computer and don't need to go to the bank.
2 The problem of the Internet is with security.
3 It isn't clear because we are not interested in who is asking, the 'doer', but in the action (asking users to register).

Vocabulary Review

Ask the students to look through the vocabulary in the box before reading. Encourage students to revise and learn any items that cause them problems.

A company's marketing department should decide what type of person will buy their product and have a ¹*customer profile* or description of the consumer in mind. Then they can design their advertisements. A good ²*advertisement* should describe the ³*features* or characteristics of the product as well as the ⁴*benefits* or advantages of buying the product.

The price of a product depends on various factors. Production costs are affected by the availability of ⁵*labour*, or workers and the availability of ⁶*raw materials* or the things needed to make the goods. How much the company has to pay the workers, or ⁷*labour costs* is another factor, and also the amount the government charges the company in ⁸*taxes*.

The people who work for a company, or the company's labour force are the company's most important asset. Many different things motivate people to work, such as ⁹*salary*, or money, ¹⁰*status* or the position they have in the company and society and the opportunity for ¹¹*social*

interaction and to meet other people. Different people like different things, and the way managers treat employees, i.e. their ¹²*styles of management* can be very important.

Grammar Review

1 Comparative adjectives

Direct students' attention first to the photos of the three hairdryers and ask them which they think will be the most expensive, which they could take on holiday, which they prefer and why.

Explain that watts are units of power, and that volts are the units of the force of an electric current. Make sure students know that mains voltage varies in different countries.

Ask students to choose one hairdryer and ask and answer the five questions about the features. They should then look at the other two hairdryers to see how they are different.

2 Ask students to go through the features and think of a benefit for one of the hairdryers for each feature.

Suggested answers:
The Vidal Sassoon will get hot more quickly than the Philips.
The Philips has more settings than the Vidal Sassoon.
The Remington can be used in the most countries.
The Remington is the cheapest.

Order of adjectives, modal verbs of probability

For the adjectives exercise you may like to prompt students with pictures or supply a list of adjectives from which they can choose.

Going to for future

You might like to elicit subject areas students could be thinking about. e.g. study, work, holidays, where they would like to live, hobbies etc. Give students enough time to prepare before they speak. This gives the students a chance to discuss their real plans and intentions.

Present passive
1 The focus is *coke*.
2 The focus is *people*.

Business Communication Review

1 Students should now have enough confidence to give a presentation on their own. Remind them to use linking devices. Give them enough time to prepare, then put them into groups of three or four. When all

students in the group have given their product presentation, they could vote on which product they would most want to buy.

2

Verbs:

↘ to decline, to decrease, to fall, to drop

↗ to improve, to rise, to increase, to grow

→ to stabilise, to maintain (position)

Nouns:

↘ a fall, a drop, a decline, a decrease

↗ a rise, an increase

3

Ask students to work alone then check their answers with a partner.

Reading

Look at the graphs below. They show the sales of eight different bikes A–H over a three-year period.

Which chart does each of sentences 1–5 describe?

Each chart is described only once.

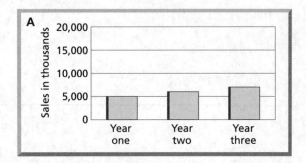

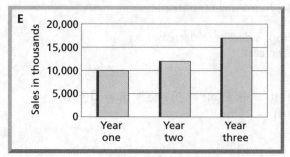

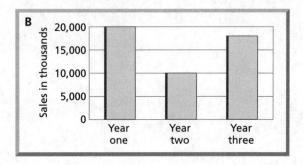

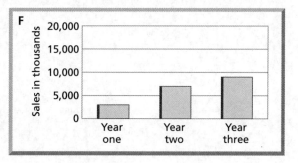

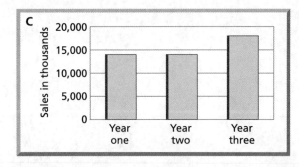

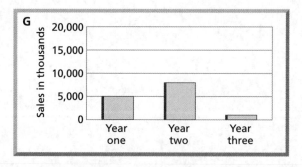

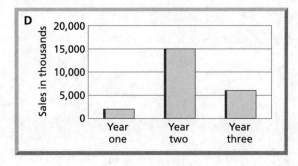

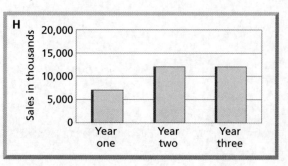

1 There was a dramatic fall in sales in year two.

2 Sales levelled out in years two and three.

3 There was a slight rise in sales each year.

4 There was a sharp drop in sales in year three.

5 Sales reached a peak in year two.

Speaking

Candidate A

Your Questions

You need to ask candidate B for this information about a company's graduate training programme.

Name of company:	_____	Business travel?	_____
Salary:	_____	Social club?	_____
Location:	_____		

Your Information

County Bank		Location	Frankfurt
Salary	£25,000	Business travel	All over Europe
Individual responsibility	No	Weekend working	No
Teamwork	Yes	Exams	Yes
Initial training	1 year	Job security	Low
Ongoing training	Yes		
Social club	Yes		

✂ ●

Speaking

Candidate B

Your Questions

You need to ask Candidate A for this information about a company's graduate training programme.

Name of company:	_____	Weekend working?	_____
Job security:	_____	Exams?	_____
Length of initial training:	_____		

Your Information

M&GB Insurance		Exams	Yes
Individual responsibility	Yes	Salary	£26,000
Initial training	6 months	Teamwork	No
Social club	No	Ongoing training	Yes
Location	London	Job security	Low
Business travel	None		
Weekend working	Sometimes		

Writing

Read the letter from a customer:

Dear Sir or Madam

Please would you send me details of the travel hairdryers which were advertised in the April edition of Hair Today.

I am particularly interested in finding a hairdryer which can use either 120 or 230 volts ac.

Yours faithfully

H Damsel (Ms)

Write a LETTER of reply to Ms Damsel (50–60 words):

- thanking her for her letter
- telling her that there is a catalogue and price list enclosed
- referring her to page 30 – details of hairdryers which use 120 or 230 volts
- hoping that she will place an order

Listening

- You will hear two telephone conversations.
- Write in one or two words or a number in the spaces provided.
- You will hear each conversation twice.

Question 1
- You will hear a woman making a booking.

RIVER TOURS
BOOKING FORM

Name (1) _____

Company (2) _____

Date (3)_____

Number of people (4) _____

Type of meal required (5) _____

Question 2
- You will hear someone ordering office furniture.

JARVIS OFFICE SUPPLIES
ORDER FORM

Customer name 1) ____Steve_____

Company 2) _____Bank_____

Order 3) _____Desks and Chairs_____

Delivery date 4) _____May_____

Delivery time 5) _____

Finance

More information about the companies mentioned in this unit is available at these websites:

> Vodaphone http://www.vodaphone.com
> Jyske http://www.jyskebank.co.uk
> Cadbury Schweppes http://cadburyschweppes.com

If your students have access to the Internet, you could ask them to do research from the company websites.

Key Vocabulary

🔲 **10.1** As a lead-in, find out if students know what the interest rate is at the moment in their country. Is this higher or lower than normal?

Read through the Key Vocabulary text with the students. Make sure that the students can pronounce as well as use the key words by playing the recorded version. You may like to use the cloze version of the Key Vocabulary text. (► page 95).

► **Further practice is available in the Workbook page 48**

Lead-in

It may be a good idea to do this activity as a team quiz with points awarded for each correct answer.

KEY:

1 All *public* companies in the UK are obliged by law to publish them. They give information on the performance of the company to the shareholders and to the public.
2 The shareholders and the taxman use this information.
3 assets = what the company owns,
   liabilities = the company's debts.
4 The shareholders are the true *owners* of the company.
5 A dividend is the share of the *profits* that the shareholders receive.
6 Turnover
7 Gross profit
8 Net profit

Language Focus One

1 and **2** Ask students to complete the questions in pairs. Elicit answers and deal with any problems saying the numbers.

KEY:

1 cardinal numbers	next numbers:	60, 75
2 ordinal numbers		4th, 5th
3 fractions		1
4 decimal numbers		1.00. 1.25
5 percentages		27%, 45%

NOTE

1 In English 0 is pronounced 'oh', the same as the letter of the alphabet except when alone before a decimal point.
2 After a decimal point figures are said individually. Thus 0.258 = "nought point two, five, eight.

Pronunciation

1 🔲 **10.2** Ask students to look though the different numbers with a partner. Play the tape with pauses for students to repeat.

2 and **3** Divide the class into students A and B. They follow the activities as directed in the Students' Book.

Language Practice One

Cardinal numbers

1 Encourage students to discuss why employers and employees feel differently about the minimum wage.

KEY:

Employers argued that the minimum wage would increase their costs. It would thus reduce profitability and would, therefore, in the long term cause unemployment.

2 🔲 **10.3** Play the tape once for students to note down the figures. Ask them to compare notes in pairs.

KEY

[1]£3.60 [2]£3.00 [3]£3.50 [4]£4.00.

3 Find out if there is a minimum wage in the students' countries and if so what it is. Encourage some discussion here on whether students think a minimum wage is a good thing.

Ordinal numbers

2 🔲 **10.4** Play the tape for students to complete the blanks. Are any of the students from cities given in the chart? Are they surprised about where any city is placed?

The Most Expensive Cities in the World		
	This year	Last year
Oslo	5	3
Zurich	6	3
Paris	7	6
Geneva	8	5
London	10	28
Stockholm	13	8
Copenhagen	14	8
Vienna	14	8
Dusseldorf	21	14
Lyon	21	15
Amsterdam	24	21
Helsinki	24	23
Frankfurt	26	26

NOTE

Statistical material like this dates fairly rapidly.

Decimals

1 Encourage students to discuss the chart.

2 🔲 10.5

KEY:

Spain 32.1, UK 22.1, Hungary 22.1, Czech Republic 19.5

1 and **2** Ask students to work in pairs and discuss the questions and then list the items in each category. Find out if students are surprised by any of the percentages.

KEY:

1 45.2%   2 18%   3 28%

4 Make sure that students complete a pie chart for their own expenditure before doing the listening activity.

TAPESCRIPT 10.6:

(**RA** = Robyn Alton, **MM** = Matthew Mead)

RA: It surprises me that people spend 22% of their income on food and drink. I spend approximately 10% of my income, erm on food and drink in a year.

MM: uh huh. I spend about 14%, I'd say, so a bit more than you, but er, less than the pie chart. It seems a lot, doesn't it?

RA: It seems a lot. What about housing?

MM: Housing; I spend about 27%, erm which is quite a lot, it's a lot of my income, er for one area, but I'm buying a second house, so it costs more money. Transport seemed quite high, I thought, er 15.7% for transport. I spend only about 6 or 7%. What about you?

RA: I spend 15% erm of my total income on transportation, er so that didn't surprise me, that figure. What about household goods and services?

MM: Well, I've only got 4%, but erm, I'm not doing much work on my house at the moment, so it's, it's not a great deal of my income. What about you?

RA: I spend 12% on household goods and services; I spend erm money on decorating, gardening erm so that's, that's a large part of my expenditure.

MM: Right. I spend about 16% – 15 or 16% on leisure goods and services, so about the same as the pie chart.

RA: That's similar to me. I spend about 15%.

MM: Right. That's on going to the gym, sports, maybe some travel.

RA: That's, that's very similar for me. What about tobacco? I've, I, I spend 0% on tobacco.

MM: Mmm. I don't smoke, so it's not an important part for me, and er 2% seems very high.

RA: It seems high to me too.

KEY:

	Matthew (male)	Robyn (female)	Pie chart
Food and drink	14%	10%	22%
Housing	27%	Not given	16%
Transport	6–7%	15%	15.2%
Household goods and services	4%	12%	14%
Leisure goods and services	15–16%	15%	16%
Tobacco	0%	0%	2%

► **For more practice see Workbook page 48**

Reading

1 Check that students understand what an offshore account is and then ask them to think of the main benefit.

KEY:

It is tax-free.

2 As a pre-reading discussion point ask your students 'Do you think trading in currencies to take advantage of exchange-rate benefits is a safe or a risky way to make money?' (It's pretty risky as exchange rates can fluctuate quite widely with very little warning).

KEY:

The No. 1 Account

3 KEY:

a = para. 4   **b** = para. 3   **c** = para. 5   **d** = para. 2

Writing

1 and **2**   Read through the text summary with the students.

3 KEY:

Same information:	To present an example:
in other words	such as
that is to say (i.e.)	for example (e.g.)
that means	

4 KEY:

1 c	2 a	3 d	4 b

➤ **For more practice see Workbook page 51**

Vocabulary

1 and **2**   Write the word *account* on the board and write *offshore* and *interest-bearing* in front of it. Ask students if they can think of any other words that can go in front of *account*. Compare with examples in the Students' Book. Then ask students to think of any words which could go after *account* (e.g. manager). Can students think of any other words that go in front of *manager*? (e.g. *Personnel, line, bank, general*, etc.)

3   Ask students to match the word partners and definitions.

KEY:

1 – f annual report	6 – h net profit
2 – i interest rate	7 – d ordinal number
3 – a investment opportunity	8 – e cardinal number
4 – j operating profit	9 – g labour cost
5 – c balance sheet	10 – b pie chart

Language Focus Two

Transitive and intransitive verbs
This may be a very good point at which to encourage the students to make more use of a good English-English dictionary, and for you to explain some of the abbreviations, etc. used in it.

1 – 4
KEY:

	Transitive/ intransitive	Simple past	Past participle	Meaning
rise	intransitive – no direct object	rose – irregular	risen – irregular	increase, go up, reach a higher level
raise	transitive – has direct object	raised – regular	raised – regular	put up, make higher
arise	intransitive – no direct object	arose – irregular	arisen – irregular	occur, appear, become evident

Pronunciation

1 🔲 **10.7a** Play the tape and ask students to number the words as they hear them.

KEY:

a = 3	b = 5	c = 1	d = 4	e = 2	f = 6

2 🔲 **10.7b** Play the recording with pauses for students to repeat the words.

3   Play the tape with pauses for students to repeat the sentences.

Language Practice Two

1   Point out that only one of the sentences in each group is grammatically correct.

KEY:

1 b	3 b	5 c
2 a	4 a	6 b

2   Ask students to complete the gap fill exercise using the correct verb and tense.

KEY:

1 rose	4 rose
2 raise	5 raised
3 arose	6 arise

➤ **For more practice see Workbook page 50**

Listening

1 and **2**
Explain to students that they are going to hear someone talking about a profit and loss account. Ask

them to work in pairs and discuss what they know about each of the points in 2.

NOTE

fixed asset: something a business owns in order to produce goods e.g. land, a building, machinery.
equity: the capital a company has from shares rather than from loans.
dividends: the profits paid to shareholders.

3 🔲 **10.8** Students should complete the summary after listening to the tape.

TAPESCRIPT 10.8:

> **Int** = Interviewer, **KJ** = Keith Jackson
>
> **Int:** Keith, can you explain what a profit and loss account is, and the main purpose of it?
>
> **KJ:** Right, well, basically it's a statement of the cash available to a company, the money available to a company, to erm, continue its operations. Erm, and it's information to managers in helping them make their decisions in running the company, and very importantly, it's information to the shareholders who are the owners of a public company – it tells shareholders how well the company is performing and how well their investment in that company is working for them.
>
> **Int:** Right, so looking at this particular profit and loss account erm, which figures would managers be most interested in?
>
> **KJ:** OK, well, turnover, for example, the first there, this should show managers the total sum of money which is coming into the company, and reading from right to left managers can see whether the company is in fact generating more or less cash year on year. Erm, now turnover is not the same as profit, of course, because it actually costs money to produce, or to run the company; so second down from turnover we look at operating profit erm, this will show what surplus, or how much money the company's making after paying for its production costs. So looking at the operating profit this should give managers the idea on how efficiently they're running the company, for example.
>
> **Int:** Right, and erm you mentioned the shareholders. Which figures are they most interested in?
>
> **KJ:** Well, looking at the example here, they, their eyes would probably go straight to the bottom line – we have the earnings per share – they would like to see how much they are earning on their investment, so the money they put into the company in the form of shares, they want to know whether they are earning more money from the company's operations. And we can see here that their earnings per share – so the money they earn on each pound they put into the company – is increasing.

KEY:

[1] a statement of the cash available to a company.
[2] make decisions.
[3] how well the company is performing.
[4] the total sum of money coming into the company
[5] generating more or less cash.
[6] how much money the company is making after paying for its production costs.
[7] how efficiently they are running the company.
[8] how much they are earning on their investment.
[9] earnings per share is increasing.

Cross-cultural Comparison

In a multinational class, try and organise students into groups with as many different nationalities as possible. In a monolingual class, encourage students to compare their own country with another one which they know well.

Business Communication

1 Divide the class into Students A and B. Student As ask Student Bs questions about the futures of the financial concerns and Student Bs reply. Ask students to give reasons for their answers.

2 Students change partners and repeat the exercise.

▶ **For more practice see Workbook page 52**

3 Give students plenty of time to prepare their roles and formulate questions. Monitor and give feedback on the board.

Final Task

Find out if students know anything about Cadbury Schweppes. This is a discussion activity which can utilise the language presented in this unit.
Ask students to discuss the questions in small groups.

NOTE

Cadbury Schweppes is a multinational beverages and confectionary company. It is both brand owner and franchisor. Popular brands include Canada Dry, A&W, Squirt, 7Up and Gini in the beverages business. The confectionary business produces chocolate and sugar confectionary. Cadbury owns Trebor and Bassett.

Checklist

1 five thousand euros, seven dollars, one point five (or: and a half) million, seven point three five, ten centimetres, fifty five percent
2 It's an off-shore account and therefore is tax-free, you can switch between currencies to take advantage of exchange rate benefits, you can even have a VISA card.
3 Turnover

Corporate Responsibility

Further information about the companies mentioned in this unit is available at these websites:

> The Co-operative Bank http://www.co-operativebank.co.uk
> Traidcraft http://www.traidcraft.co.uk

If your students have access to the Internet, you could ask them to do research from the company websites.

Key Vocabulary

🔲 **11.1** As a lead-in, find out if any of the students refuse to buy certain products, for example if the product has been tested on animals.

Read through the Key Vocabulary text with the students. Make sure that they can pronounce as well as use the key words by playing the recorded version. You may like to use the cloze version of the Key Vocabulary text. (▶ page 96)

▶ **For more practice see Workbook page 53**

Lead-in

1 Read through the responsibilities with the students and ask them to tick the responsibilities that they think a company should have. Then compare their answers in pairs.

2 KEY:
The following are suggestions:

1 – c/e	4 – c	7 – e
2 – f	5 – b/d/g	8 – b/d
3 – c/e/a	6 – g/a	

Language Focus One

1 Ask students to study the box, and focus on the difference in structure of the 'if' and 'main' clauses.

2 🔲 **11.2** Allow the students time to complete their answers then play the tape for them to check.

KEY / TAPESCRIPT 11.2:

(**CH** = CleanHome Manager, **MC** = Management Consultant)

CH: What'll happen <u>if</u> our profits fall?
MC: <u>If</u> your profits fall the shareholders' dividend <u>will</u> decrease.
CH: If our shareholders' dividend decreases they'll be very unhappy.
MC: Yes, your situation <u>might</u> be very serious if the public loses confidence in the company.

CH: Our share price might fall if people <u>lose</u> confidence. I think we should consider this matter seriously.

3 KEY

1 Conditional 1 sentences are made up of **two** clauses.
2 The main clause describes **consequence**.
3 The 'if' clause describes a **situation or event**.
4 It is not important which clause comes first.
5 In the main clause use **will + infinitive**.
6 In the 'if' clause use if + **present tense**.
7 We **can** use 'might' instead of 'will' if we are not sure about the consequence.
8 Short forms of will and will not are **often** used in spoken conditional.

Language Practice One

1 KEY:
1 If a company conducts irresponsible marketing, customers won't buy its products.
2 A small company will go out of business if its customers don't pay on time.
3 Many customers won't buy products if companies test them on animals.
4 If a multinational company pays 'first world' prices for goods from developing countries those suppliers will become self-sufficient.
5 If a company delays payment, what will the consequences be?

Pronunciation

2 KEY:
1 Will and will not are pronounced as their short forms – 'll and won't
2 In the question form, will is pronounced as its long form – will

3 Read through the policy statements with the students. Check they understand *needlessly* and point out the definitions given underneath the statements.

KEY:

1 c	2 d	3 b	4 a

4 After completing this exercise, ask students to discuss what they think of the company's policies in general, and would they choose it because of these policies?

KEY:

(Suggestions)

a The Cooperative Bank will not invest your money in countries if they deny most of their people human rights.

b If companies' activities are needlessly harmful to the environment, The Cooperative Bank will not invest your money in them.

c The Cooperative Bank will not invest your money in companies if they test cosmetics on animals.

d The Cooperative Bank will not invest your money in companies if they export armaments to oppressive regimes.

► **For more practice see Workbook page 54**

Reading

Remind students about the problem of late payment and find out if it is a problem in students' countries.

1 KEY:
1 pays late   2 has the right

2 KEY:
Finland = 24 days   Germany = 38 days   UK = 50 days

3 KEY:
1 Small businesses are doubtful because the same legislation in Europe is not effective.
2 In Italy the average length of time companies wait for payment is 84 days.
3 The Federation will use the new law to raise awareness.
4 It will soon publish a league table of the worst payers in order to 'name and shame' them.

5 Ask the students to read the text and complete the chart.

Problem:	big companies taking too long to pay (up to **90** days)
The solution:	Main customer solved problem when it **gave staff credit cards**.
Situation now:	Most corporate customers now pay in **30** days.
Amount now owed:	£5,000

Vocabulary

1

KEY:	
Creditors (person waiting for money)	**Debtors** (person who owes money)
1 to charge interest 4 to submit/send in an invoice 7 to make a mistake on the invoice 9 to be owed money 10 to overcharge	2 to pay late 3 to settle/pay an invoice 5 to pay by credit card 6 to use delaying tactics 8 to take ages to pay

3 KEY:
1 to charge interest
2 pay late
3 made a mistake   to overcharge
4 delaying tactics
5 am owed
6 taking ages to pay   pay an invoice
7 by credit card.   to submit an invoice

Cross-cultural Comparison

Allow time for the discussion. Try to ensure that some of the Key Vocabulary is used. The topics may cause quite a polemic, and there is no 'right' answer.

Language Focus Two

1 and **2** Read through the examples and the information with the students.

1 KEY:
1 *consider* is followed by a gerund
2 *agree* is followed by *to* + infinitive
3 *must* is followed by infinitive without *to*

2 KEY:
Group A = verb + gerund
Group B = verb + *to* + infinitive
Group C = verb + infinitive without *to*

► **For more practice see Workbook page 55**

Language Practice Two

1 Explain that the two columns give different points of view about whether companies are responsible. Students complete the gaps using the correct form of the verb in brackets.

KEY:

1 conducting	7 to improve
2 to preserve	8 giving
3 providing	9 to change
4 to raise	10 producing
5 to introduce	11 do
6 make	

2 This pair work is designed to get students using the gerund/infinitive rather than to exchange opinions.

Listening

1 Before listening, students discuss the three statements. Find out which statement most students agree with.

2 💬 **11.4a** Play the first part of the interview. Elicit which of the views in 1 he agrees with.

TAPESCRIPT 11.4a:

Int = Interviewer, **KM** = Kevin Manton

Int: Kevin, can I ask you – do you think big business behaves responsibly?

KM: Erm, the simple answer is no, no I don't think it behaves responsibly, erm I think that it's not the job of a business to behave responsibly, it's the job of a business to make money, and I think they always put making money as their top priority before the effects of what, of, of their actions on people and environment.

KEY:

He agrees with statement 3.

3 💬 **11.4** Check that students understand:
factory farming – controversial but productive farming where animals are kept inside in small cages
sweatshop – a small business or factory where workers are in bad conditions and paid very low wages
phosphates – chemicals widely used in industry and as a fertiliser
free-range – from animals allowed to move around in a large enclosed area

TAPESCRIPT 11.4:

Int: Kevin, can I ask you – do you think big business behaves responsibly?

KM: Erm, the simple answer is no, no I don't think it behaves responsibly, erm I think that it's not the job of a business to behave responsibly, it's the job of a business to make money, and I think they always put making money as their top priority before the effects of what, of, of their actions on people and environment.

Int: Can you give me some examples of, of how they don't think about people and the environment?

KM: Certainly. Erm, for example factory farming is very bad for the environment, but it makes erm factory farming companies very high profits; erm, companies aren't concerned about the destruction of the rain forest and they're often not concerned about the conditions their workers work in.

Int: Erm, thinking about that then; are there any products that you don't buy?

KM: Well I, I never buy meat that I know comes from a factory farm; erm, I never buy clothing that I know's been made in a sweatshop or with child labour; erm I always try not to buy products that have been tested on animals – I check the labels in the shop to make sure they haven't been tested on animals, and I never buy anything from a company that I know invests heavily in a country where the government abuses human rights of the people who live there.

Int: OK. Well, looking at the other side of the coin, are there any products that you do try to buy?

KM: Well, I, I always try to buy erm, cleaning things, you know like washing up liquid, that I know contain very low levels of phosphates, because phosphates kill fish in rivers; erm, I usually buy Traidcraft coffee, erm, it's from Oxfam and it helps people in developing countries, and I always buy free-range eggs – they taste nicer as well.

KEY:

1
- factory farming
- destruction of the rain forest
- working conditions

2
- meat from a factory farm
- clothes from a sweatshop or made with child labour
- products that have been tested on animals
- products from companies that invest in countries where the government abuses the human rights of the people who live there

3
- cleaning agents (e.g. washing up liquid) with low levels of phosphates, because phosphates kill fish in rivers
- Traidcraft coffee from Oxfam, because it helps people in developing countries
- free-range eggs because all other eggs are the product of factory farming and they taste nicer as well

Writing

1 and **2** Read through the texts with the students.

KEY:

1 They'll face bankruptcy and they may grow the coca plant for cocaine.
2 Cafédirect pays the growers a fair price.
3 Either they get paid a fair price for their coffee, or they face bankruptcy…

3 KEY:
1 more focused on social problems.
2 because they are 'ethical consumers' and want to help improve the economy and situation of the workers in underdeveloped countries.
3 The company lacks <u>neither</u> customers <u>nor</u> workers.
4 No, the company does not lack workers. It does not lack customers either.

4 KEY:
Sentence A shows that there is a quantity of two.
Sentence B shows that there are two possible options.
Sentence C shows that both options are excluded.

The students can now do questions 5 and 6.

5 KEY:
1 either or
2 neither nor
3 either or
4 Both and

6 KEY:
1 Neither Cafédirect nor Traidcraft wants to harm the environment.
2 Both Cafédirect and Traidcraft are socially responsible companies.
3 We can offer either to deliver all the goods next Wednesday or we can send part of the order today and the rest next week.
4 Either we can withdraw from the market totally or we can concentrate our efforts on a small sector.
5 Both Brian and Alec's application for the job is very strong. It's a difficult decision
6 Either Latin American coffee growers can sell their coffee beans to Cafédirect or they can grow the coca plant for cocaine.
7 Neither Traidcraft nor Cafédirect finds it difficult to recruit voluntary staff.

► **For more practice see Workbook page 56**

Business Communication

1 Draw students attention to the Traidcraft advertisement and ask them to complete the job specification. Check students understand *liaison*.

KEY:

POSITION:	Product Manager
Product(s):	Gifts and Homeware
Responsibilities:	various aspects of Product Management
Qualifications:	degree in Marketing or similar
Experience:	one or two years in product management
Benefits:	flexible hours and pension scheme

Final Task

Ask students to work in pairs. Find out what experience your students have of negotiating both at work and in other situations. For a successful negotiation, both parties must be satisfied with the result.

When they finish negotiating, ask students to compare the 'result' with the other students who had the same role. Who got the best deal? Did any of the negotiations fail?

Checklist

1 Yes
2 to make a profit for the shareholders
  to treat employees well
  to pay other companies on time for services/goods used.
3 refuse: *to* + infinitive
  consider: gerund
  could: infinitive without *to*
4 a Yes
  b Yes
5 If you ... I'll ...

Competition

Further information about the companies mentioned in this unit can be found at these websites.

> Pepsi http://www.pepsiworld.com
> Coca-Cola http://www.cocacola.com

If your students have access to the Internet, you could ask them to do research from the company websites.

Key Vocabulary

🔲 **12.1** If students are already working, find out who their companies' main competitors are.
Read through the Key Vocabulary text with the students. Make sure that they can pronounce as well as use the key words by playing the recorded version.

You may like to use the cloze version of the Key Vocabulary text. (▶ page 96)

▶ **For more practice see Workbook page 58**

Lead-in

1 – 3 Before discussing the questions, check students can pronounce compe'tition, com'petitor, com'petitive. Students discuss in small groups.

2 KEY:

sportswear: Nike, Adidas, Reebok, ...
fashion: Gap, Next, Versace, Gucci, ...
cars: Ford, Toyota, VW, Rover, Renault, ...
telecommunications: Cable and Wireless, Telcom, AT&T
computers: Apple Macintosh, IBM, Dell, Hewlett Packard, ...

3 KEY:

- offer a better product than their rivals
- keep the price right for the market/offer a lower price than their rivals
- use clever advertising/marketing that appeals to the target market
- use catchy tunes or jingles that people remember (e.g. Coca-Cola's 'Just for the Taste of it).
- develop an easily recognisable image for the product (e.g. Pepsi's change to the colour blue in the 1990s).
- promote the brand image (in 1990 a survey in 11 countries of 6,000 brands showed Coca-Cola to be the most powerful and successful brand name in the world)
- sponsor someone very famous to endorse the product (e.g. Michael Jordan for Nike trainers)
- develop tie-ins with other providers (e.g. Coca-Cola's biggest customer is McDonald's)
- make sure that merchandising has a positive effect on the brand's image

Language Focus One

Check that students understand the following expressions before they read the passage: demerger, float (on stock exchange).

1 KEY:

| 1 | b | 2 | c | 3 | a |

2 KEY:

| 1 formed | 2 retained | 3 split |

3 KEY:

It has split the Asian and central European bottlers in order to exploit the growth in the European market.

Pronunciation One

1 🔲 **12.2**

NOTE Stress changes depending on the context. The strong form is to add emphasis to the verb have. The weak form is used when have is not the focus of the sentence, e.g. We have bought two hundred shares in their company. – The emphasis is on the two hundred and have is therefore not important.

Language Practice One

1 Check that students understand sponsor sports events. Monitor and check that students are pronouncing has and have correctly.

KEY:		
	Student A	**Student B**
increase sales	Yes, by 5%	Yes, by 4.5%
attract new customers	Yes, 200,000 new customers	Yes, 220,000 customers
maintain customer loyalty	Yes	Yes
enter new markets	Taiwan, Korea	Mexico, Czech Republic
introduce ethical policy	No, but going to	Yes
update code of practice	Yes	No, but going to
send employees on training courses	Yes	Yes
sponsor sports events	No	Yes. Local football team

Student A scores 2, 1, 1, 1, 0, 2, 1, 0 = 8
Student B scores 1, 2, 1, 1, 2, 0, 1, 2 = 10

▶ **For more practice see Workbook page 58**

Reading

For the first question the students do not need to read the text. Direct them to the illustration over the page only.

1 The illustration shows Coca-Cola and Pepsi in fierce competition for world domination. Each company is trying to paint the world with its own colours.

2 Ask the students to guess the answers and then to scan the text quickly to see if they were correct.

KEY:

1 – c   2 – d   3 – b   4 – a

4 At the time the article was written, Eastern Europe and the former Soviet Union were newly opened markets. Today, China is the biggest potential new market.

5 The next questions demand closer reading.

KEY:

1
a 1897 – Coca-Cola began operating outside the USA
b 1943 – Eisenhower sent a cable to Washington asking for 3m bottles of Coca-Cola
c 1959 – the Chairman of Pepsi gave Soviet President Kruschev a bottle of Pepsi as cameras clicked
d 1972 – Brezhnev gave Pepsi the exclusive right to sell cola in the Soviet Union
e 1989 – The Berlin Wall between capitalist West Germany and communist East Germany collapsed, leading to German reunification
2
a 3:1 – Coke sells three times more than Pepsi outside the USA
b 41%–32% ratio – Coca-Cola has 41% of the US cola market and Pepsi has 32%
c 80% – the amount of operating profit Coca-Cola earns from its overseas beverage (drinks) business
d $2.5 billion – Coca-Cola's profit last year
e $112 million – Pepsi's profit last year
f 60 – the number of Coke bottling plants the military built outside the USA to supply their soldiers
g 28%–33% – the improvement in Pepsi's profits in Mexico during the last two years
h $750 million – the amount Pepsi has invested in Mexico in order to double the capacity of its factories there
i 720 – the number of litres of soft drinks that the average American drinks each year

6 KEY
1 It was written in the mid 1990s. This is clear from references to eastern Germany as 'new markets'
2 The market for Coke and Pepsi has probably significantly expanded by the opening up of China as a new market.
3 It seems very unlikely.

Vocabulary

Word groups: competition
1 KEY:
All of them refer to the stronger competitor.

2 KEY:
Both Coca-Cola and Pepsi want to [1]claim the lead in the race, to [2]outsell the rival's products in order [3]to gain supremacy.

Compound nouns and adjectives

1 Ask the students to highlight the words in the text. Compound nouns and adjectives are made up of two parts. Sometimes these parts are separated by a hyphen and sometimes not. There is no hard and fast rule about this. Encourage students to check in their dictionary if unsure.

2 KEY:
a best-known – adjective – most famous
b trademark – noun – a logo or symbol used by a manufacturer to identify and advertise his/her goods
c snack-food – noun – food eaten for a quick and convenient meal or between meals
d overseas – adjective – abroad, to a foreign country
e soft-drinks – noun – sweet, cold drinks
f chairman – noun – the most senior person in the company

3 KEY:
1 overseas   3 soft-drinks   5 best-known
2 snack-food   4 trademark   6 chairman

Cross-cultural Comparison

This is an open discussion about the two companies.

Listening

1 🔲 12.3a Direct students to the three expressions. Ask students to guess what they think the expressions mean. Play recording 12.3a then check answers as a class.

TAPESCRIPT 12.3a:

Int = Interviewer, **KJ** = Keith Jackson

Int: The global market place is very competitive; how can a company become a market leader?

KJ: Well I think basically by having a good product and using good marketing. But to become a market leader there are three main strategies, I think – cost, so reducing cost, producing more cheaply, selling more cheaply; er differentiation – that is making your products appear very special in the market place, and innovation – so finding new products and new ways to market products, which is particularly important in the, as you said, the global market.

KEY:

1 Cost focus – reducing costs, of production and the selling price
2 Differentiation – making your products seem very special in the market place
3 Innovation – finding new products and ways to market them

2 🔲 **12.3b** Play the tape once for students to write down the strategy. Then, play the tape again to note down the details.

TAPESCRIPT 12.3b:

Int: Can we take a concrete example and look at the soft drinks market? Can you explain how these three factors work?

KJ: (Fine), well if you look at erm, cost as focus, or a cost-focus strategy, erm let's take cola for example, erm we know that big supermarket chains in the UK – Safeways or Tesco's or Sainsbury's – they produce their own cola at low cost and can sell it more cheaply than Coca-Cola, for example. Erm differentiation, I mean, a good example is, I think, Tango; they've managed to penetrate the market and be competitive by using a very interesting and rather wacky advertising campaign for their product. Erm, and innovation, for example, Virgin we know of as er a music or airline company; they also own cinemas, and through the cinemas, the distribution channel of their cinemas, they've managed now to promote their own version of cola, so they've ... innovation in controlling distribution means they can be competitive in the cola market, for example.

KEY:		
Company	Strategy?	How they employed the strategy
1 Safeway Tesco Sainsbury's	cost-focus strategy	by producing their own cola at low cost and selling it more cheaply than Coca-Cola
2 Tango	differentiation	by using a very interesting and 'wacky' advertising campaign
3 Virgin Cola	innovation	by controlling the distribution channel for their cola (through their cinemas)

3

TAPESCRIPT 12.3c:

Int: Keith you mentioned erm, some very famous names there, erm, companies which compete in the global market place. Are there any particular problems faced by companies who, who wish to be competitive in a global market?

KJ: Well yes there are. I mentioned Virgin and Coca-Cola for example, these are global players in the soft drinks market, erm they do face particular problems. We could take another example – McDonald's in the food retail business. For example McDonald's, the main part of their selling strategy is the quality of their products, the standardised quality. It's very difficult for a company to control or guarantee the quality of their product on a global scale. Erm particularly where they have to be sensitive to or adapt to local cultures and customer expectations. A good example with regard to McDonald's is the fact that they do not sell *beef* burgers, so burgers made of beef, in India, for example, because that would possibly offend local cultures there. Of course globally marketing becomes a particular problem – can companies erm communicate the same or a similar standardised message about their product in different language regions of the world? And McDonald's we know are very lucky in this respect because they have a good product in the sense that the product they offer is recognised among a large population, youthful population of the world as symbolising the American lifestyle, for example, so McDonald's are very lucky in the power of the product and the message they have on a global scale. Other companies of course have much greater difficulties with their products.

KEY:

1 Quality: highly standardised
2 Local culture and customer expectations: sensitive and adaptable – e.g. no beef in India.
3 Marketing: their product is recognised globally as a youthful symbol of the American lifestyle.
4 The product: McDonald's is very lucky in the power of the product and the message they have on a global scale.

Language Focus Two

1 Read through the text with the students and then direct them to the questions.

KEY:

1 Yes
2 Yes
3 a *since*
  b *for*
4a *since* 1967
  b *for* a long time
  c *since* December
  d *for* three weeks
  e *for* a month

82

Pronunciation Two

📼 **12.4** Play the tape. Elicit how *for* is pronounced. Play the tape again with pauses for students to repeat the sentences.

Language Practice Two

1 To demonstrate the task, do the first sentence as a class then ask students to complete the sentences in pairs.

KEY:

1 has had ... since
2 has been ... since
3 has had ... since
4 have been ... for
5 has outsold ... since
6 have produced ... for
7 hasn't changed ... since

2 For this exercise encourage as many statements about the differences as possible.

3 You could leave this to do as a warm up exercise at the beginning of the next lesson to see how much students can remember about the present perfect.

➤ **For more practice see Workbook page 60**

Writing

1 Check that students understand the expression *competitive edge*. Ask the students to complete the quiz, then discuss their answers in pairs. Ask them to give advice to their partner (*you should ..., you ought to ...*).

2 Read through the guidelines on CV writing. Students prepare their own CV. Students compare in pairs and make suggestions for any improvements.

Business Communication

1 Match the illustrations with the quotes. Ask students to discuss the experiences in pairs. Do they think any of the techniques were unacceptable?

2 Ask students to put the stages of an interview into a logical sequence. Point out that there might be some differences. The following is the most likely; accept small, logical variations.
e, g, c, b, f, h, a, d, i

3 Read through the example as a class. Point out that they don't need to write anything for **f** and **h**. Ask students to practise their exchanges – prepare in pairs and then change and practise with another student.

4 📼 **12.5** Now play the cassette and ask the students to complete the task.

TAPESCRIPT 12.5:

Int: So Brett. What do you think your strengths are?
Brett: Well, I enjoy working with people as part of a team. I think the best results come from working together. I've found that's true in all the projects I've worked on.

Int: Well, Barry. You seem to have done lots of different things. How have you found the time for them all?
Barry: I am just very active. I try to organise my studies and my other interests so I can do as many things as possible. I think it's good to meet lots of different people and have lots of different experiences.

Int: Why do you want to work in this area?
Julie: I think marketing's a really interesting area. I've really enjoyed doing my marketing course and it's convinced me that this is the right area.

KEY:

What the candidate said to 'sell' him/herself:

Brett   I think the best results come from working together.
Barry   I am very active. I try to organise my studies and my other interests so that I can do as many different things as possible.
Julie   I think marketing is a really interesting area. I've really enjoyed doing my marketing course.

You could point out that Julie and Barry should give more examples.

Final Task

Ask students to discuss in pairs or small groups.

Checklist

2 present perfect
3 past simple
4 *for* is used to show the starting point of the action
5 *since* is used when considering the time between the start and now

Review 4

Finance, Corporate Responsibility and Competition

Business Review

Ask the students to read the text and discuss the questions in small groups. You may like to explain the pun in the title (i.e. that it is both ethically sound and tastes delicious). Check the topics as a class and elicit which unit topics the questions cover.

> **Heavenly Chocolate**
>
> The Fairtrade chocolate bar 'Divine' is made from West African cocoa beans, grown by farmers who own a one third share in the company and receive a Fairtrade premium for their produce. One taster asked 'is it Cadbury's?' which pleased Twin, the company who make 'Divine'. Twin also own Cafédirect Fairtrade coffee, which showed a 55% growth in sales last year.

Question 1 reviews the topic of corporate responsibility. Questions 2 and 4 review the topic of competition and question 3 reviews talking about profitability and trends (units 9 and 10).

1 The cocoa bean farmers are paid 'first world' prices for their product.
2 Because the product tasted as good as their main competitor's.
3 It's very healthy (it showed a 55% growth in sales last year). Ethical consumerism is becoming more and more popular.
4 Chocolate – Cadbury's, Nestlé, etc. Coffee – Nescafé, etc. If the market for Fairtrade coffee grew so rapidly last year, they should be worried, as it will inevitably take market share from them.

Vocabulary Review

1 Ask the students to list the words under the correct headings.

KEY:		
Finance	**Corporate Responsibility**	**Competition**
1 interest rate	8 payment on time	4 market share
2 annual report	9 ethical consumers	11 enter new markets
3 rise	10 product policy	12 market leader
5 offshore bank account	15 society	16 global market
6 profit and loss account	20 environment	17 open market
7 financial results		19 competitors
13 tax year		
14 turnover		
18 fall		

2 The definitions can be found in the vocabulary sections of units 10, 11 and 12.

3 This could be done as a timed competition. Accept any words that they can recall.

Grammar Review

1 **Talking about figures and Conditional 1**
Ask the students to read the text and look at the pie chart. Ask students what the chart shows, and which is the most important new market.

2
NOTE 1 billion = 1000 million.
1 The total size of Coca-Cola's potential new market is 5.442 billion.
2 China, India and Africa. The total size of these is 2.608 billion.
3 China = 22%   India = 15%   Africa = 10%
4 Problems might include, for example, low disposable income (so low price needed), availability of raw materials, economic re-structuring in China, poor infrastructure (affecting transportation), low levels of international trade, lack of information technology for computerised systems.
Accept any other sensible suggestion.
5 Pricing no more than the market will bear; whether these countries need the product, etc.
6 Probably Pepsi-Cola and possibly local equivalents.
7 Approximately 35%

8 Selling more to the same people/attracting new customers/getting customers to switch from other brands.

3 Can the students remember how to write a correct conditional sentence?
1 If Coca-Cola <u>increases</u> its present market by 1.9 billion consumers, it<u>'ll be</u> the most powerful soft drinks brand in the world.
2 If Coca-Cola <u>promotes</u> itself successfully in China its market share <u>will grow</u> by around 20%.
3 If Coca-Cola <u>markets</u> itself in China it<u>'ll</u> have to sell more to earn the same profit as it earns in America because prices will be much lower.
4 If consumption per person <u>is</u> as high in its new markets as in its current markets, the company <u>will</u> have to open many more bottling plants.
5 If the population in North America and Europe <u>continues</u> to shrink Coca-Cola <u>will</u> have to enter new markets in order to keep its profits high.

4 **Present perfect/gerunds and infinitives**
Can the students recall the uses of the present perfect and how to use gerunds and infinitives?
1 Some investors <u>have stopped investing</u> in companies which are involved in weapons production.
2 Some consumers <u>avoid dealing with</u> companies which are involved in animal testing.
3 Ethical investors <u>choose not to be involved with</u> companies which have links with certain political regimes.
4 Ethical investors <u>prefer to deal with</u> companies which bring a direct benefit to society or the environment.
5 Some consumers <u>choose to invest</u> in companies which contribute to a sustainable future.

Writing Review

Re-phrasing and exemplifying, transitive and intransitive verbs
1 Raise is a <u>transitive</u> verb, <u>in other words/that means/that is to say</u> it is followed by a direct object.
2 Rise is an <u>intransitive</u> verb <u>in other words/that means/that is to say</u> it is not followed by a direct object.
3 <u>Intransitive</u> verbs, <u>such as/for example/for instance</u> *rise, fall, bargain, compete, respond* are not followed by a direct object.
4 <u>Transitive</u> verbs, <u>such as/for example/for instance</u> *pay, publish, expect, spend* are followed by a direct object.
5 <u>Transitive</u> verbs, <u>in other words/that means/that is to say</u> verbs that are followed by a direct object, form different sentence patterns to intransitive verbs.
6 <u>Intransitive verbs</u>, in other words verbs that are not followed by a direct object, form different sentence patterns to <u>transitive</u> verbs.

You may like to ask the students to write some sentences using *rise, raise* and *arise*.

Reading

Read the advertisement below for The Theta Business Travel Organiser.

Are sentences 1–6 below right or wrong?

If there is not enough information to answer 'right' or 'wrong', choose 'doesn't say'.

THE THETA BUSINESS TRAVEL ORGANISER FROM EPSILON COMMUNICATION SYSTEMS.
This is the electronic organiser for every business traveller.

The Theta is connected to the Epsilon Satellite communication system, which means that when you travel abroad the Theta automatically changes its time as you travel.

The Theta knows which country you are in and can display all the local information you need at the touch of a button. This includes currency conversions, city maps, useful phrases, local customs and political and financial background. All at no extra charge.

It will adjust all your phone numbers so that when you look up a number, it will display the correct international dialling codes.

As well as being the most useful organiser for the business traveller, the Theta is also small and light and is adaptable to all the main office information systems. It comes with a lifetime guarantee and a smart leather holder.

Email NOW to receive a Theta FREE for a month and experience the convenience of the Theta next time you travel.

Epicom.co.uk

		Right	Wrong	Doesn't say
1	The Theta is made by Epsilon Communication Systems			
2	The Theta is the cheapest organiser available.			
3	It is possible to have a Theta free for one month.			
4	The Theta is also a phone.			
5	The Theta can help the business traveller with language problems.			
6	You have to pay extra for the local information service.			
7	The Theta has a five-year guarantee.			

Speaking

Candidate A

You need to ask Candidate B for this information about a company's record for corporate responsibility.

Your Questions

Company name: _____		Environmental record: _____
Equal opportunities for minority groups: _____		Environmental record: _____
Good working conditions in Europe: _____		

Your Information

PCF Minerals

Investments in countries with poor human rights records	Yes	Good working conditions in Europe	No
		Pay rates for workers	C
Equal opportunities for women	Yes	Use child labour	No
Equal opportunities for minority groups	No	Environmental record	C
Allow trade unions	No	Payment on time	D

A = excellent, B = good, C = average, D = poor, E= bad

Speaking

Candidate B

You need to ask Candidate A for this information about a company's record for corporate responsibility.

Your Questions

Company name: _____		Use child labour: _____
Equal opportunities for women: _____		Pay rates for workers: _____
Investments in countries with poor human rights record: _____		

Your Information

Sunshine Foods

Investments in countries with poor human rights records	No	Good working conditions in Europe	No
		Pay rates for workers	B
Equal opportunities for women	Yes	Use child labour	No
Equal opportunities for minority groups	Yes	Environmental record	B
Allow trade unions	No	Payment on time	A

A = excellent, B = good, C = average, D = poor, E= bad

PHOTOCOPIABLE

Writing

You are head of Information Technology at your company's headquarters.

It is 1.00 p.m. and your assistant is at lunch. You have received an urgent request to go to the Marketing Department to solve a computer problem they are having.

Write an e-mail for your assistant, telling her:

• where you are

• when you will be back

and asking her to meet the visitors who are due at 2.30.

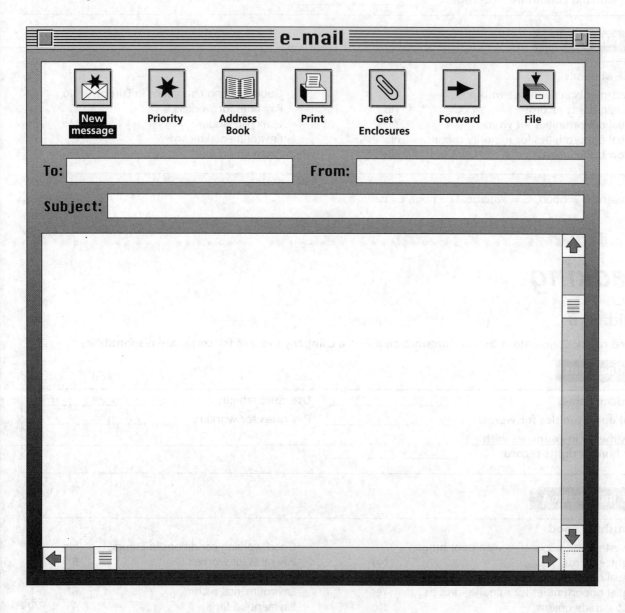

© Pearson Education Limited PHOTOCOPIABLE

Listening

Listen to this conversation between a safety inspector and a manager of a factory.

- For questions 1–8 choose the correct phrase to complete each sentence.
- Mark one letter a, b, or c for the phrase you choose.
- You will hear the conversation twice.

1 How many inspectors visited the buildings?

a 3

b 4

c 5

2 Which area has got the biggest safety problems?

a production

b transport

c the warehouse

3 When the inspector tells the manager where the problems are, how does the manager feel?

a not surprised

b surprised

c happy

4 Bob Jenkins is

a the Warehouse Manager

b a warehouse worker

c a safety officer

5 A lot of workers

a have got safety clothes but do not wear them

b have not got safety clothes

c do not know about safety clothes

6 Some of the fire-fighting equipment is

a too expensive

b the wrong type

c broken

7 Some of the fire doors

a are open

b cannot be opened

c are used too often

8 The inspector

a will be back after Christmas

b wants to see the secretary now

c wants to warn the officials

Answer Key

Reading

1 b   **2** a   **3** c   **4** b   **5** b

Speaking

This shows the information that each student is required to obtain.

Candidate A

Address:	346 Park Street, London W4
Name of Manager:	M. Peters
Conference room:	Yes
E-mail:	Hoteurostar.co.uk
Restaurant facilities :	Yes

Candidate B

Location:	35 Westgate Street, Edinburgh
Fax Number:	0131 682 2772
Restaurant:	Yes
Car hire:	Yes
Conference room:	Yes

Writing

WISLEY PURCHASE ORDER			
QUANTITY	PRODUCT REQUIRED	PRICE	POSTAGE AND PACKING
six	siteasy chair	£19.99 each £39.98 for 3	£ 12.50
		TOTAL	**£92.46**

Listening

Question 1	c	museum
Question 2	b	platform 10
Question 3	1	15th December
	2	7 courts
	3	75 metres
	4	1,500 brochures

Answer Key

Reading

1 Card E **2** Card A **3** Card C **4** Card B **5** Card D
6 Card G

Speaking

This shows the information that each student is required to obtain.

Candidate A

Name:	Fizz Co.
Products:	soft drinks
Nationality:	British
Profit last year:	£16,360,000
Number of employees:	7,250

Candidate B

Name:	European Business Press
Business:	books about business
Owners:	International Press Ltd.
Offices:	London, Paris, Rome
Plans:	**to** re-structure

Writing

To:	Marcia Auger
From:	xxxxxxxx
Date:	xx/xx/xx
Subject:	Computer training

· ·

As you know I will be attending a computer training course tomorrow from 10.00 a.m. to 3.00 p.m.

I will be back in the office at 3.30p.m., but will not be able to attend your lunch-time meeting.

Please present my apologies.

Thanks

(*initials*)

This sample answers gives all the information that the students were asked to include. Students are not expected to produce language at this level to pass the exam.

Listening

Question 1 a £10
Question 2 b theatre.
Question 3 1 24th
　　　　　　　　2 8 a.m.
　　　　　　　　3 4 Production Supervisors
　　　　　　　　4 10.30 a.m.

Answer Key

Reading

1=B,   2=H,   3=A,   4=G,   5=D

Speaking

This shows the information that each student is required to obtain.

Candidate A

Name of company:	M&GB Insurance
Salary:	£26,000
Social Club:	No
Location:	London
Business travel:	No

Candidate B

Name of company:	County Bank
Salary:	£25,000
Initial training:	One year
Weekend working:	No
Exams:	Yes

Listening

QUESTION 1

1 BAILEY
2 London Bank
3 24th November
4 20
5 Lunch

BEC test 3 part 2

QUESTION 2

1 HUMPHRYS
2 London
3 15 desks,   20 chairs
4 27th May
5 9.00

Writing

This sample answer gives all the information that the students were asked to include. Students are not expected to produce language at this level to pass the exam.

> Manto Electrics
> 45 Park Industrial Estate
> Chelmsby
> Essex
> CM5 7FK
> 26 April 2000
>
> Ms H Damsel
> 46 Rose Lane
> Colforth
> Norfolk
> NO2 5JL
>
> Dear Ms Damsel
>
> Thank you for your letter and your interest in our range of hair care appliances.
>
> Please find enclosed a copy of our latest catalogue and price list. Details of our products, which work at 120 or 230 volts, are given on page 30.
>
> We look forward to receiving your order soon.
>
> Yours sincerely
>
> P. Mitchell

Answer Key

Reading

1 Right 2 Doesn't say 3 Right 4 Wrong
5 Right 6 Wrong 7 Wrong

Speaking

This shows the information that each student is required to obtain.

Candidate A

Company name:	Sunshine Foods
Equal opportunities for minority groups:	Yes
Good working conditions in Europe:	No
Environmental record:	Good
Payment on time:	Excellent

Candidate B

Company name:	PCF Minerals
Equal opportunities for women:	Yes
Investments in countries with poor human rights records:	Yes
Use child labour:	No
Pay rates for workers:	Average

Writing

> Amanda,
>
> I've gone to the Marketing Department to deal with an urgent computer problem. I'll be back by 3 p.m.
>
> Could you meet the visitors from Newtel at 2.30, and entertain them until I return? Please apologise for my absence.
>
> Thanks,
>
> (Bernie)

This sample answer gives all the information that the students were asked to include. Students are not expected to produce language at this level to pass the exam.

Listening

1 b
2 c
3 b
4 a
5 a
6 c
7 b
8 a

Key Vocabulary Cloze

Key Vocabulary One

Companies need _____ Some companies provide _____ such as clothes, cars and food. Other companies provide _____, for example insurance, banking, information technology or training.

Companies want _____, in other words, customers to buy from them again and again. To win _____, many companies have a _____, or set of rules, for _____. The code of practice explains what the customer can expect of the company. Customers can complain about the _____ they receive (the way staff deal with them) and the goods they buy.

Key Vocabulary Two

Companies are involved in many activities, for example, _____ _____ _____ and _____, in a range of different industries, such as _____, _____, _____ and _____. Many well-known companies are _____, these are companies which _____ in a number of countries.

Multinationals often have a complicated structure. There is usually a _____ or _____. This company owns other companies or parts of other companies. These other companies are called _____.

Key Vocabulary Three

Business today is international. Business people often have to travel a lot. They have to plan an _____ for a _____ to make good use of their time. On a business trip people may meet _____ and business partners for the first time. It is usual for colleagues from different countries to experience _____. In other words, they may be surprised by foreign _____, that is, the different ways that other _____ or different _____ do things.

Key Vocabulary Four

Sometimes _____ realise that they are not achieving their _____ or objectives effectively, that is they are not getting the results they need. In this case they have to re-plan their _____. It can be useful to get an outsider, e.g. a _____ to analyse the company's performance and recommend changes to make it more efficient. A _____ can be useful, that is, an analysis of the company's strengths (S) and weaknesses (W) and also of the opportunities (O) and threats (T) that face the company. _____, or solving problems, is a necessary part of running a company.

Key Vocabulary Cloze

Key Vocabulary Five

Companies often include details about their history in their marketing literature, their annual reports and company presentations, in order to show that they are _____ and have _____ in their field. This can include information about the _____ or person who started the company, and _____ and _____ in the company history.

Key Vocabulary Six

Retailing is the provision of _____ or _____ to the customer. _____ buy goods directly from the _____ or from a _____ (the middleman), and make their income from the _____, or difference, between the price they pay for the goods and the price they sell the goods at to the _____. A _____ is the place where customers can purchase goods, for example, a _____ or a _____. Nowadays, many customers are shopping from home: shopping by _____, _____ or _____ is becoming very popular.

Key Vocabulary Seven

For nearly every type of _____ there are many similar goods on the market. The _____ of a product are the things that make it special and different from other similar products. A good _____, which brings the product to the public's attention, should describe these USPs. The marketing department should have a _____ in mind, that is the sort of person who will buy the product. When trying to sell a product, it's important to give information about the product's _____ or characteristics, and to emphasise the _____ or advantages of the product to the customer.

Key Vocabulary Eight

Most people work because they need to earn a _____ but money is not the only _____ or reason why people work. People get _____ from different factors, such as _____ with colleagues. _____, that is your professional position, and _____, doing something well, can be important. Some companies really value their employees and see them as the company's main _____. Managing people well can lead to better results and _____ for the company, but this can be difficult to do. People respond differently to different _____. Some organisations give their workers freedom to develop their roles and others don't.

Key Vocabulary Cloze

Key Vocabulary Nine

All businesses are affected by their immediate environment. Many factors influence them, for example, _____ (that is how easy or difficult it is to find workers); _____ (how much it costs to wmploy people), and _____, such as oil and wood. The amount of money a company has to pay the government in _____ is another factor. Businesses are also affected by the _____. In a period of _____, many businesses suffer, their profits fall and they have to make _____. In this climate there will be a rise in _____. These factors can affect sales and prices, and change the _____, or direction they move in.

Key Vocabulary Ten

Companies and individuals often borrow money, and it is important to find a favourable _____. Rates are variable, and can _____ depending on the market. Many _____, (people who use their money to earn more money), choose foreign or _____ because they are tax-free. Anyone can buy shares in a _____ and become a shareholder. All public companies in the UK are obliged by law to publish their _____ at the end of the _____. They do this in their _____ to _____. Annual reports include _____ which show _____, or the total sum of money which is coming into the company.

Key Vocabulary Eleven

Market research shows that many consumers are _____; they expect the companies they buy from to behave responsibly. Most ethical consumers have high _____ so companies usually listen to them and will promise, for example, not to use child labour or to pollute the environment. A recent report showed that many companies have an _____ which covers areas such as _____, _____ and the environment. Some companies have a policy of paying _____ prices for _____ goods from developing countries – they pay more because they think the workers and the economies of developing countries need support.

Key Vocabulary Twelve

In an _____ any number of sellers or _____ can offer goods for sale. An efficient producer, who keeps costs low, can set a low price for goods that other companies find it difficult to _____ with. All companies try to gain the biggest _____ possible, and compete aggressively with their _____ to do this. Companies with the biggest market share for a product, the _____, may compete with their rivals on quality, image, brand loyalty or price. Major companies compete across borders in the _____ and try to _____, in countries where they do not have a presence.

96